# DEMI MOORE

# DEMI MOORE

## The Most Powerful Woman in Hollywood

## Nigel Goodall

MAINSTREAM
PUBLISHING

EDINBURGH AND LONDON

## ILLUSTRATIONS

The author and publisher are grateful to All Action and Corbis picture libraries for use of the photographic material.

Copyright ©Nigel Goodall, 2000
All rights reserved
The moral right of the author has been asserted

First published in Great Britain in 2000 by
MAINSTREAM PUBLISHING COMPANY (EDINBURGH) LTD
7 Albany Street
Edinburgh EH1 3UG

ISBN 1 84018 269 5

A catalogue record for this book is available from the British Library

Typeset in Plantin
Printed and bound in Great Britain by
Creative Print and Design Wales

*To Sue, Simon and Louise, with gratitude.*
*This one is for you.*

Nigel Goodall is a British-born journalist, broadcaster and author with a dozen books to his credit, including *Johnny Depp* and the best-selling, prize-nominated Winona Ryder biography. He has also written dozens of articles for magazines, contributed to various album and video projects, and is a regular showbusiness contributor for independent radio covering a wide variety of stories including the Golden Globe and Oscar ceremonies.

Born in Folkestone, Kent, he studied history, English literature and art at St George's School in Tunbridge Wells. He had been married for twenty years before his divorce in 1992, and has two children, both now in their early twenties. He is also an actor for drama groups in Sussex where he now lives.

# CONTENTS

# AUTHOR'S
# NOTE

*'The moment one begins to investigate the truth of the
simplest facts which one has accepted as true, it is as
though one had stepped off a firm narrow path into a
bog of quicksand – every step one takes one steps deeper
into the bog of uncertainty'*
LEONARD WOOLF

This is a story of fame. It is a story of celebrity and its con-
sequences. There are no villains here, no twisted plots and no
whodunit ending. Although Demi Moore may well be the most
photographed, written about and talked about Hollywood star,
she is also in many ways the most misunderstood, both because
of our ever-increasing rush to judge and, perhaps more to the
point, simply because she appears to be so well known.

The British historian Richard Holmes describes the biographer
as 'a sort of tramp permanently knocking at the kitchen window
and secretly hoping he might be invited in for supper'. That is

probably true. It was for me in the fact that I wanted to tell a story that Holmes would have described as one leading to 'a relationship of trust' between biographer and subject. Although I did not have the opportunity to get to know Demi Moore personally, trust is always what one seeks whether authorised or not. As Holmes correctly states: 'The possibility of error is constant in all biography.' I think it is important therefore to clarify that Demi Moore was not interviewed for this book, and has in no way co-operated with or participated in the preparation of this biography. She has neither endorsed nor authorised its contents.

That is why I would like to suggest that this work, like any other, is a beginning and not an end, an invitation to inquiry, not an attempt at foreclosure. So much of what becomes a story, whether formally or merely in the relating of a dinner-table anecdote, is based upon verbal shorthand, metaphorical leaps of faith and an interpretation of the facts. But facts can change, and new interpretations can at any moment alter our perception of them.

There is another reason for suggesting that this is *my* story of Demi Moore. It cannot be *the* story of Demi Moore. There is no such thing; even autobiography (or perhaps autobiography most of all) represents an editing of the facts, a selection of detail, an attempt to make sense of the various, arbitrary developments of someone's real life. In the end, there should be nothing shocking about human existence, because whatever has occurred is simply human. If I have succeeded in my aim, I have given the reader the tools to create his or her own portrait of Demi Moore, the opportunity to reinvent and reinterpret, within the broad context of a particular time and place, the life of a remarkable actress and woman, the highest-paid of her time, and probably the most powerful of her generation.

# ACKNOWLEDGEMENTS

Many dozens of people made *Demi Moore: The Most Powerful Woman in Hollywood* possible. First and foremost all those unnamed who agreed to be interviewed and gave me so much of their time. Thanks also to my publisher Bill Campbell and his colleagues at Mainstream and to Caroline Budge, my editorial co-ordinator, for nursing me through it; to the eminently wise Adam Parfitt for his suggestions; Keith Hayward, whom every writer should have as their researcher (but mercifully don't); Kjell Gunnarsson at Demi Moore Org who did his best to satisfy my demands for information; Nick White and all at the British Film Institute Library and Archive in London who gave much-needed assistance with scripts and production notes; Sally Thomason at Blockbuster Entertainment (my local video store at Pevensey) for the endless supply of Demi's movies, and Graham Taggart for very kindly lending me cassettes of *Wisdom* and *The Seventh Sign*. Thanks, too, to my 'sometimes' agent, Robert Smith, for his continued support, and to Kelli Whiting for the phonecalls.

Among my friends and colleagues who provided advice, practical information, help and encouragement in various combinations were: Simon Russell, Caroline Osborn, Mike Derrick, Sarah Edwards, Jonathan and Sue Terry, John Highfield, Tim Bowden, Karen Terry, Tim Spray, Elizabeth Cunningham, Bob and Chris Costen, Scott and Ana Coldwell, Neil Milner, Anne Sprinks, Peter Lewry, Simon and Louise Groves, Peter Sinclair, Sue Baverstock, and of course my children, Adam and Kim, who as always cared and shared. Many film company press offices also helped unstintingly; among them, I am most grateful to Lawrence Atkinson at Buena Vista (UK) and Georgina Partridge at Entertainment Films (UK); and Tracy Lopez at Columbia-Tristar for her help on another project. It would be remiss of me not to mention Roy Galloway at Eastbourne's town centre Curzon Cineplex for his tireless hospitality every time one of my books is published, and Shawn Derry in Florida for creating and maintaining my website.

I would also like to thank for their often unsung research efforts those who maintain the following internet sites: Demi Moore Org; Demi Moore Unofficial Homepage; The Unofficial Site For Demi Moore; the Amazing Demi Moore Gossip Page; Hollywood Online; E! Online; People Online; The Journal On-line; Chicago Tribune; Discovery Channel Online; Demophonic Home Page; Save The Earth Magazine Online; The Smoking Gun Archive; Mr Showbiz; the Internet Movie Database as well as the Yahoo, Excite and Deja.Com search engines.

I would also like to thank the following magazines and news-papers for their coverage of Demi over the years, all of which I consulted during my research: *LA Daily News* (formerly *Valley News*); *Los Angeles Herald Examiner*; *Chicago Sun-Times*;

*Interview*; *Now*; *National Enquirer*; *Moviegoer*; *Seventeen*; *OK!*; *Variety*; *Screen International*; *The Globe*; *Daily Mail*; *The Sun*; *Empire*; *People Weekly*; *Premiere*; *Washington Post*; *In Style*; *Film Review*; *Vanity Fair*; *Sky*; *TV & Satellite Week*; *Sight and Sound*; *Radio Times*; *Flicks*; *Marie-Claire*; *Cinemania* and *Cable Guide*. Thanks also to all the journalists who have interviewed Demi, and whose articles formed a valuable part of my research.

I am also indebted to several books: *Hollywood: The New Generation* by James Cameron-Wilson (Batsford, 1997); *The Virgin Encyclopedia of the Movies* (Virgin Books, 1995); *Chronicle of the Cinema* (Dorling Kindersley, 1995); and the immensely helpful *Bruce Willis: The Unauthorised Biography* by John Parker (Virgin, 1997).

And finally thanks to Demi Moore and her publicist, Pat Kingsley, who responded to my request for an interview and co-operation in such a straightforward and uncomplicated way when any other star of her magnitude, I feel sure, would have unleashed publicists and pitbull lawyers. Ms Kingsley's office at PMK, in contrast, simply suggested I continue with my book, but without their help. And for that I thank her. It probably forced me to work harder than an official biographer might. I hope she discovers that her trust has been rewarded with a book that accurately and fairly sums up Demi's life and career so far.

# DECONSTRUCTING DEMI

*'The truth is you can have a great marriage, but there are still no guarantees'*

DEMI MOORE

There are times in everybody's life when, suddenly and inexplicably, everything seems to go wrong. As Demi Moore neared her thirty-sixth birthday on 11 November 1998, she was closer to that state than she had ever felt before. She kept on going, simply because she didn't know what else to do. But other people might have given in and had a breakdown.

Enduring the attentions of the gutter press, as she had done throughout her career, she would probably have admitted that she went through much of the previous three months feeling tired, tense and not very happy, emotions only intensified by the knowledge that, just a week before, the end of her marriage to Bruce Willis had been announced publicly after years of speculation.

As well as having to deal with the break-up of her marriage, Demi was still coming to terms with the death from cancer and a brain tumour of her mother that July. Virginia Guynes, aged fifty-four, according to *USA Today*, had been ill for some time, and although Demi had had little contact with her in recent years, 'the two reconciled late last year when Moore learned of her mother's illness. The actress, along with her three daughters, had spent the last three months at her mother's home in Farmington, New Mexico, taking care of Guynes, and was by her side when she died.'

According to the article, Willis joined Demi and his daughters in New Mexico shortly after they had, somewhat surprisingly, attended the Florida première of Willis's latest film *Armageddon* that same week. 'He was expected to attend the small, very private, relatives-only funeral for Guynes on Monday night, the 13th,' reported the paper.

Virginia Guynes could never have been described as a conventional parent, and the world in which she lived was scarcely typical either. She had, over the years, accelerated a criminal record with a long history of drug and alcohol abuse, being arrested at different times for, among other things, drink driving and arson. It was tragically ironic that years before Virginia's last fatal illness, Demi had been trying repeatedly 'to get help for her troubled mother, unsuccessfully enrolling her into a substance-abuse programme before finally severing contact'.

The already difficult relationship between mother and daughter had deteriorated further when Guynes had accused Demi of 'not taking care of me' to the many journalists to whom she related damaging stories about her daughter. The situation wasn't helped by Virginia posing naked in *High Society* magazine, deliberately imitating Demi's infamous pregnant ones from *Vanity Fair* two years before. When *Playboy* magazine passed on the idea for a naked spread of Virginia the following year, Guynes blamed her daughter's interference, commenting sulkily that 'Demi's paraded her naked body three times in magazines, but just because her mother gets the chance to earn some modelling money, she has to stop it'.

Two years before her death, however, she confessed to the *Albuquerque Journal* that she had finally shaken her drinking problems and was now sober. It was, she said at the time, 'all that Demi had ever wanted'.

The tabloid press, for once, were treading carefully. They had to. Just six months earlier, Demi and Bruce announced that they were seeking $5 million damages from *The Star* and the Australian women's magazine, *New Idea*, in a libel suit for articles both publications had run the previous year, in which it was claimed that their marriage was on the rocks, 'secretly heading for splitsville, and now turning into Hollywood's nastiest divorce in years'. As far as the Willises were concerned, it was both defamatory and generally damaging overall. 'We're not filing this lawsuit for financial gain but to protect our reputation,' Bruce insisted.

Another article, three weeks later, had gone even further, reporting that Demi 'partied up a storm' with actor Johnny Depp after he broke up with Kate Moss. Not only that, but the article depicted Bruce and Demi as a couple deep in marital discord, made worse by their apparent drifting apart, cheating on each other and alienated behaviour. *New Idea* covered 'Demi's Bulimia Hell' in which the magazine discussed the actress's obsession with exercise and suggested she had an eating disorder that was driving the couple apart.

Even more damaging was the *National Enquirer*'s suggestion that Demi had allegedly become romantically involved – albeit briefly – with *Titanic* heart-throb Leonardo DiCaprio after he was photographed leaving the Willises' $3 million white stucco mansion on the beach in Malibu the morning after they had spent a romantic day together on the streets of Los Angeles.

Even if she had fucked him, that was it. That was the end. The gossip-columnists had gone too far – and there was no way they were going to get away with it this time.

Being Hollywood, of course, there was no shortage of other equally irate celebrities. Jim Carrey, for instance, had just announced legal proceedings over an article in another Australian magazine, *Woman's Day*, which had alleged that he had sexually harassed Jennifer Tilly, Courtney Cox, Alicia Silverstone, Drew Barrymore and Courtney Love.

Although they had, for the most part of their careers, ignored the tattle, refusing even to dignify such tales with a response, 'Bruce Willis, Demi Moore and Jim Carrey all intend to pursue their legal rights vigorously and we are confident of vindication,' said a spokesperson of the law firm representing them.

*New Idea*'s editors eventually retracted their story and printed a full-page apology for 'any hurt and embarrassment suffered by the couple as a result of the article', for which they also acknowledged there was no foundation, and unconditionally withdrew their suggestions.

But as if to prove that when it rains it pours, Demi and Bruce were also facing another setback. If that last battle had been against a familiar enemy, the tabloid press, their next one was fought with a new one: their nanny Kim Tannahill.

The case, filed on 28 January of that same year, in the US

District Court in Idaho, stated that Tannahill had been taken on as the nanny for their newborn third child, Tallulah Belle, in March 1994. As a condition of her employment she was required to sign a confidentiality agreement in keeping with California law. It is where Tannahill reckoned she spent a third of her time, another third in Idaho, and the remainder elsewhere. That 'elsewhere', she later told lawyers, would engage her in extensive travelling throughout the United States and the world over the ensuing three and a half years. It was a period that witnessed the busiest and most lucrative periods of her employers' careers.

It was also a period that ended for Tannahill on 29 August 1997 when she was fired for being, the Willises claimed in their suit, a 'dishonest and disloyal employee, who, among other things, misappropriated moneys, improperly billed personal expenses to the Willises' accounts, failed to follow instructions, and, on occasion, improperly performed her duties in dealing with the children.' On top of that, according to *E! Online* on the internet, the court papers listed the allegations that Tannahill 'had violated a non-disclosure clause in her contract, had purportedly racked up numerous, unauthorised charges on the Willises' credit cards, and finally had failed to make good on an $8,000 loan that Bruce and Demi made her.'

But rather than plan her defence, continued the internet report, Tannahill countersued, filing a complaint on 8 February 1998 in Los Angeles Superior Court for civil-rights violations, fraud and deceit, assault, false imprisonment, stalking and invasion of privacy. In her suit, she claimed the Willises were inattentive toward their children, and Moore's prescription-drug use caused her to become 'extremely paranoid, delusional, temperamental and obsessive.' She was, she charged, 'literally whisked away and required to engage in extensive travelling throughout the US and the world', that her social life was ruined as the Willises refused to allow visits from her boyfriend and family, and that she was forced to work 'seven days a week and 24 hours a day' with no overtime. In an attempt to collect the overtime wages that she claimed she was owed, Tannahill filed a separate action in a Los Angeles federal court.

She also took out a libel action against the *National Enquirer* for running what she termed 'a scathing article' under the headline 'DEMI, BRUCE AND THE SEX-CRAZED NANNY – THE UNTOLD STORY' in which the tabloid reported that Tannahill had flirted with Willis, was nowhere to be seen when the couple's eldest daughter nearly drowned or when the youngest fell and broke her arm. Among other things, complained her suit, prepared by former Idaho Attorney-General David Leroy, the article had depicted Tannahill as neglectful, vindictive and drug-influenced in both her private and domestic working life. Even more damaging in this was the accusation that the Willises had retaliated to her earlier claims by arranging the story and providing home photographs to illustrate it.

According to Martin Singer, the attorney acting for Bruce and Demi, the claims were 'gratuitous nonsense' and just a response to his clients' own lawsuit. The allegations, he added, were 'absolutely without merit. Any number of current and ex-employees will confirm that the allegations made by Mrs Tannahill are without merit. I can't make it any clearer [than that]. She made these claims in an effort to extort money from my clients'.

And presumably he was right. At the January hearing, US

District Judge B. Lynn Winmill ruled in the Willises' favour prohibiting Tannahill from disclosing to anyone any personal information she had gained about the family, and later on 13 April, Judge Audrey B. Collins in California threw out Tannahill's federal labour-violations complaint saying federal court was the wrong jurisdiction.

By this time, of course, Demi's life with Bruce Willis was ending. It was something that Kim Tannhill had also claimed in her lawsuit, that their marriage was clearly 'on the rocks' by June 1997. They rarely saw one another any more, and although they kept up appearances when they went out together in public, they didn't actually go out that much. From that alone, it was apparent the couple had begun to drift apart. They may have shared the same home, but they didn't share the same life. It was just the beginning of what would be a painful end to one of Hollywood's most high-profile couples.

Making matters worse was the difficulty they found in maintaining a relationship amidst successful careers and punishing work schedules that kept them separated much of the time. Constant rumours that both partners had been stepping out with others only added fuel to the fire. And although for the most part they ignored the gossip, the stories rattled on, sometimes even touching on accusations of each having temperamental personalities with roving eyes for their co-stars, rowing furiously with each other, and not even being together any more. Although they would most probably both admit that the gossip hurt, they were also aware of how persuasive some of those stories could be.

There was, for instance, the rumour from as far back as 1990 that Willis had been angry over Demi's intimate scenes with

Patrick Swayze in *Ghost* – and at one time, during filming, had even marched on to the set with a baseball bat. There was also her alleged fling, while Bruce was away filming, with DiCaprio, of course, and, two months after that, in August 1997, she was supposedly spotted 'dirty dancing', as one observer put it, with a string of young men at a fashionable Beverly Hills restaurant, including gyrating seductively with Madonna's brother, Christopher Ciccone. A few days after that, she was reportedly seen again dancing on top of a New York bar, this time with no bra and the outline of her breasts clearly visible.

On the other hand, Bruce Willis, once described as a woman-ising party animal, wasn't quite so blameless. Lisa Comtaruk was a dark-haired, twenty-six-year-old Demi look-alike who had met Willis a year earlier. She was also a former employee of his Valley Entertainment company and had, according to *The Star*, told a pal that she had been having a secret affair with the actor right up until two weeks before the end of his marriage. There were also the Hollywood star-spotters at the 1998 Cannes Film Festival who were quick to observe that Bruce Willis looked a lot closer to Milla Jovovitch, his co-star in *Fifth Element*, than two people who just happened to be promoting a movie together. It was much the same story the following year when, with Demi out of town, he was linked to another of his leading ladies, this time Liv Tyler from *Armageddon*, who was even headlined in the *National Enquirer* as 'THE BEAUTY THAT BROKE UP BRUCE AND DEMI'. But that, according to Tyler's former manager, Bebe Buell, was ridiculous. 'It is so unfair to Liv and her boyfriend, Joaquin Phoenix. It is unfair to Bruce as well. Besides, Liv's father [Aerosmith frontman Steven Tyler, whose band contributed several songs to the movie soundtrack] was at the première in Florida and if he had thought there was anything going on, he would have kicked Bruce's ass.' And later, in another issue of the same tabloid, was the story of how Willis had apparently 'turned his back on Demi after she suffered a devastating miscarriage'. She was, the article claimed 'eight to nine weeks pregnant with the couple's fourth child – and what they hoped would be be their first son – when she lost the baby'.

When it did finally happen and an announcement was made that the marriage was over, most Hollywood insiders simply shrugged and said, 'Who cares?' to themselves. There were others, though, who wanted to add their own spin on the news. One of those ubiquitous 'friends' who always seem on hand to comment on showbiz affairs of the heart revealed that the end of their relationship had left both partners inconsolable. Willis is supposed to have said: 'It's a very sad day for me, and I would just like to be on my own for a little while.' He would even skip the première of his latest film *Armageddon*, and cancel a Hollywood 'Walk of Fame' ceremony in his honour. Demi, according to journalist Liz Smith, 'was taking the break-up much harder than Bruce. She is one unhappy lady'.

Another of those friends spoke to the *New York Daily News*: 'I think they came to a hard decision. They intend on doing it amicably, but [whether they can manage it] remains to be seen. It's been over for a while. They were hanging in there to see if they could put their marriage back together. Partly they've been lazy because they didn't want to deal with the numbers – Bruce especially. He's hunkering down. He doesn't want to part with a lot of money.'

With all the attendant touring and publicity duties that movie-making entails, and their own spare time at a premium as they

threw themselves deeper and deeper into their Hollywood schedules, it seems their relationship didn't really stand a chance.

When Demi read the news about Lisa Comtaruk, she was
reported to be devastated and furious. It was then that her upset
turned into a public display of anger. She immediately
dispatched a crew of workmen to a warehouse in downtown
Hailey where they would spend the entire day removing some of
Bruce's most prized possessions. 'They were at it for hours,' said
one source, according to *The Star*. 'Right on Main Street, hauling
box after box of furnishings and the sound equipment from
Bruce's old nightclub, The Mint, out of her building and across
the street into an abandoned building he owns. Demi was livid.
Up until then, she was considering Bruce's pleas for
reconciliation.' Not even the £60,000 pair of diamond earrings
that he bought her in New York, or the advice of their mutual
friend and Bruce's co-star Michelle Pfeiffer on the set of *The
Story of Us* (ironically about a couple going through a
separation), or their reunion for that Christmas under the pleas
of their three daughters, Rumer, Scout and Tallulah Belle, could
help.

Aside from the fact that the couple held off from making the
announcement of their break-up until their daughters' school
had closed for the summer, no other explanation was offered.
Neither were details of who was likely to have custody of the
three girls, or whether it was a temporary separation or a
divorce. Nor was there any word on how they might divide their
substantial assets which included properties in Malibu,
California, a fourteen-room pied-à-terre on Central Park West in
New York City, their spread at Idaho, the large chunk of Penns
Court in New Jersey, the mass of other real estate and, of course,

their partnership in the Planet Hollywood restaurant chain, despite the fact that the company was reported to be spinning off its axis amidst apparent financial trouble in August 1999. There was even talk about a potential voluntary bankruptcy filing that if all went according to plan, would allow the company to continue operating while it restructured. According to Jerry Jackson of *The Orlando Sentinel* on the internet, the bankruptcy filing was then the latest in a series of dramatic tumbles. Film producer and co-founder Keith Barish had resigned the previous March as a board member after selling nearly half his stock. Then in June 1999, making matters worse, former president, William Baumhauer resigned, less than a year after joining the company.

Even more damaging were the claims in *Business Week* by unnamed memorabilia collectors that some of the so-called authentic costumes, model and assorted knicknacks are not so authentic, despite denials by the Planet Hollywood execs who said they are. Neither were they trying to pull movie-magic trickery on customers. Although they confirmed there are no more than five replicas in each restaurant and are clearly labelled as such, the collectors remained peeved because, if they were fakes, then they would cut into the going price for the originals.

Trickery, or not, with no pre-nuptial agreement or divorce papers filed, then or since, it seemed for the time being, at least, Bruce and Demi would continue with business as usual – only now, it would be separately.

# FROM SOAP TO MOVIE STAR

*'Marriage was a goal. A family for me as a young girl was*
*my image of what I hoped for. It was part of the big picture'*
DEMI MOORE

Demi Moore had been taking chances since her early teens and had
come through most of them pretty much unscathed. Born on 11
November 1962 in the New Mexico town of Roswell (the former
trailer-park settlement where Fox Mulder and others believe aliens
had landed two decades earlier), almost two hundred miles west of
Lubbock, Texas, Demetria Gene Guynes (Demi for short,
pronounced 'Dem-ee' – her mother named her after a brand of
shampoo she'd spotted in a magazine), grew up believing herself to
be the daughter of teenage parents: Danny Guynes, an often un-
employed salesman of advertising space in newspapers, and a
heavy-drinking mother, Virginia. Money was a rarity that drifted in
and out of their lives. When it was out, they simply made do; and
when it was in, it was usually squandered on gambling and alcohol.

By her own admission, Demi had a deprived and chaotic childhood. Faced throughout much of it by poverty, alcoholism and domestic abuse, she reckoned that the family must have moved house, on average, at least every six months from the time she was five until she left home at sixteen. But that, she said, was 'one element of my childhood that was really a positive asset for me. By moving a lot, I learned to assimilate into whatever new surroundings I found myself in and to become very comfortable with people quickly. I think that was one of the strongest contributing factors to my becoming an actor, because I constantly had to readjust, even reinvent. But at the same time, it also became very easy for me not to become attached to people, places or things. I learned to enjoy people and places for the time I had, for the moment, to be in the moment, and to move on.'

As well as that, she continued, 'I think it gave me an internal strength, because I was comfortable doing whatever I had to do. Being alone, being new, being faced with the unknown didn't paralyse my existence.'

For much of her childhood, Demi surrounded herself with dolls. One of her favourites was a large monkey with a half-peeled plastic banana in his hand. 'My mother said I had it until it was falling apart, ragged and loved to destruction. One Christmas my parents got me a new one, and I unwrapped it and I saw the old one, new one, old one, new one. My mother said I ran out of the house with the new one and I came back without it, and they never found it.' Today, though, she has a replica. She came across it in a shop 'and knew immediately it was just like the one I had when I was little'. She likes to believe it's the same one, only resurfaced.

Equally redolent of her childhood days was Donny Osmond's

hit record 'Puppy Love', the smell of White Shoulders (her mother's favourite perfume) and banana pudding with vanilla wafers.

With good memories and bad, her childhood, she acknowledges, was complicated: 'I had an essence in my life that I was nothing.' This idea was brought home forcibly to her in the difficulties she encountered fitting in at each new school – something which, because of her parents' nomadic existence, she had to endure at least twice a year. Quiet and withdrawn, visibly nervous and unsettled, she was, as she puts it, a skinny, bespectacled, 'cross-eyed clumsy ugly duckling'. With her hair cut boyishly short, she probably felt slightly ostracised as well. 'I was always kind of nerdy,' she said. 'Even when I did blossom in some other ways, there's that feeling that you still carry around. It was always about what everybody else was into, so that I could fit in.'

She was very self-conscious about her right eye, which crossed over slightly. One of the first things she did when she was able to afford it was to have the problem surgically corrected, which apparently took at least two attempts. Even going through that was better, she thought, than the black pirate's eye-patch she had worn 'trying to correct it' naturally. (In the years which followed she would often be rumoured to have undergone other cosmetic surgery – to remove excess fat from her hips, stomach and buttocks and, on another occasion, to enlarge her breasts, and then reduce them again. She kept a dignified silence on the whole subject. But it was made worse by the Hollywood star-spotters who insisted one breast was higher than the other.)

Looking back on her formative years, all she could do was wish that things had been more settled; and even though 'there were bad times in my childhood', she said with understatement, 'there were some really good times in there as well. I wasn't afforded the luxury to live it with the idea that it was painful or fearful, because I needed to be only strong, so that I could survive it.'

Most unsettling, perhaps, was the period when Danny walked out on them. Demi was thirteen. He was, she has since described, a self-destructive, gambling con-artist. From this point on, she would be the mainstay in her mother's now even more unstable life. Her parents divorced, and by the early 1970s when Los Angeles seemed the most glamorous place in the world, she and Virginia were renting a small apartment in West Hollywood. Although it was the first seemingly permanent home since the trailer-parks that had featured so much in her mother's and her own upbringing, it was still not what Demi craved.

It was only after Danny left them that the teenager learned he was not her biological father, and that she was the product of one of her mother's earlier and hushed-up liaisons. She had found the Guyneses' marriage certificate in a drawer. It showed they were married on 19 February 1962, barely nine months before she was born. When she went to visit an aunt in Texas two years later, she discovered the truth. Her real father, Charles Harmon, an Air Force officer, married and dumped by her mother all in the space of two months, had, when he heard of Demi's birth, tried to make contact; Virginia, however, refused to allow him back into her life. He had never seen a photograph of his daughter, and didn't even know what she looked like until he visited her briefly at her aunt's house, an encounter which Demi described as 'a bizarre experience' and one she apparently never repeated. By all accounts, the discovery about Danny hit her very badly. As far as she was concerned, her mother's cover-up was nothing less than a 'tremendous betrayal', especially when she realised that all her relatives knew the truth.

Once Danny left, Demi would hardly see him again before he committed suicide just before her seventeenth birthday. He had inhaled the carbon-monoxide fumes from the exhaust of his car. Living alone with her mother in the seedy low-rent apartment-building (shared, among others, with the still newly emerging Natassja Kinski, who was also living with her mother), the parent-daughter roles became reversed.

(She and Kinski rehearsed scripts together and was, Demi remembers, 'only about two years older than me. There was something really incredible [about her] because there's certainly something much more sensual about European women, they're encouraged to be much more open with their sexuality. I could see the effect that she was having on people and I think she revealed to me something that I wanted to do but was keeping a secret.'

While her mother's drink problem overwhelmed her own emotional troubles, it didn't seem likely that she was going to get the opportunity to act. Well, not right away, anyway. Although she attended Fairfax High School in west Los Angeles, she admits that she just drifted through her classes much of the time, gritting her teeth and learning to put up with it until, unable to stomach it any more, she decided to alter the course of her schooling – and her career. She would simply drop out of both school and her mother's house. At that point, she was barely sixteen, a teenager on the very fringe of Beverly Hills, like a child looking through the window of a sweet shop. But Los Angeles was full of kids in her position – on the periphery of the phoney atmosphere of a city where the wealth and opulence enjoyed by a minute segment provided the inspiration and ambition of the rest.

Although she had no money, Demi managed to hook up with the graduate crowd which was then reliving the golden days of Timothy Leary's 'tune in, turn on and drop out' era, an era that had kicked off the counterculture rebellion of the 1960s long before it was fashionable to be a social renegade, and was the hallmark of the decade in which free thinking, free love and free drugs were the buzzwords of a generation.

Leary himself, of course, was a key figure of that period. Kicked out of West Point military academy and dismissed from Harvard as well, his adventures with hallucinogenic drugs earned him both notoriety and imprisonment, but he never repented. Even in his mid-seventies, several years before his death, he repeated his belief that 'psycho-active brain-activating drugs are the most powerful tools humanity has for operating your mind, your brain, developing new language, building upon communications, new cultures and subcultures'. Attracting followers of his teachings, like a cult leader, Leary, (incidentally, Winona Ryder's godfather) was a true visionary. Bound up in those visions was the dream of change, enfranchisement and a new dawn of freedom that flavoured the 1960s even as America became mired more and more deeply in the Vietnam War. 'The long history of psychedelic drugs,' Leary taught, 'has always been associated with shamanism, mysticism, art, poetry, free sexuality, acceptance of the body, an ecological sense of the oneness of all things. This runs through Hinduism, Taoism, Buddhism and Greek humanism. There was an enormous drug influence on the French Revolution, on Wordsworth, Coleridge, Emerson and Thoreau. It's a tradition.'

It was, of course, ironic that early into the decade that followed, marijuana had become the dope of childhood; older kids got through school on alcohol or other stimulants such as amphetamines and Quaaludes, more commonly known as pep and diet pills, uppers and downers. And it was in these surroundings that Demi's own ambitions began to take shape. She was drawn, through necessity, to that candy-store window of Hollywood, first as a model and then trying for bit-parts in film and television.

At sixteen, she had spoken three words on TV and now sought greater exposure, literally, by agreeing to pose provocatively and wearing practically nothing for a freelance photographer who got her on the front cover of the titillating men's magazine *Oui*, plus a spread inside. It did not, however, provide her with the big break she had hoped for. Nor did the period she spent modelling around Europe. In fact, she remained as anonymous as the thousands of other girls trying for the same lucky break. Not to be discouraged, Demi survived on small, irregular roles on daytime television soap operas which she interspersed with casual work as a telephone debt-chaser. It seemed she had the ability to make her husky voice sound menacing.

She was firmly in the wild-man arena when she met rock musician Freddy Moore, then pushing twenty-eight, who played in a going-nowhere band called The Kats in the clubs and bars of Los Angeles. 'I wanted him,' Demi admits. 'And there was the added adrenaline rush from the fact that he was married.' But she probably fell in love with Moore's band long before she fell for him. Like The Replacements and Soul Asylum, The Kats hailed from Minneapolis where, with founder members Dennis Peters and Al Galles, Moore was born and raised and attended the University of Minnesota during the late 1960s. It was the period when Richard Nixon had just been inaugurated as President, The Beatles (whose first hit was released just five weeks before Demi was born) were still together, and America was waging war in Vietnam.

The band had been around for years under a variety of names, gigging continually at some of Bob Dylan's old haunts, mainly coffee houses in the Dinkytown and Westbank areas of Minneapolis. It was here, in what is still one of the Midwest's most beautiful locations, that Peters and Galles first hooked up with Moore. A decade later, still playing together, they headed for Hollywood. There, performing as The Kats for the first time, they cut several records, made a video for MTV and even got their names into the *Who's Who of Rock 'n' Roll* before eventually disbanding.

According to Freddy, a former pupil of California's Novato High School and Richfield in Minnesota, he and Demi moved in together after their second date. He went home and told Lucy, his partner of ten years, that he was leaving. And Demi – already with her new borrowed stage name – did much the same to her boyfriend, Tom, who promptly threatened to beat up Freddy if he ever set eyes on him, not realising that it was she who had engineered the affair in the first place.

Freddy and Demi married a year or so later, in February 1980, and in between collaborated on writing three songs: the lyric of 'It's Not a Rumour', and both the lyrics and music for 'Changing' and 'Heat'. The fact that they could work together so well so quickly was a reflection of how their relationship had erupted almost out of the blue. 'He was an amazing performer,' Demi bragged. This view was confirmed by the *Los Angeles*

*Herald Examiner* when the band appeared at a club called The Whisky in 1979. 'He begins hopping his little body around the stage the instant the spotlights hits him,' wrote rock critic Ken Tucker. 'And, once started, he never stops. He pops his eyes, flails his arms and bends his fingers in time to the beat, acts out his songs with gestures so broad they become visual puns, and leaps into the audience literally to collar an innocent patron into loving him.'

But, sighed Demi, he was 'a very different person off stage than on – like Clark Kent and Superman'.

Looking back with some bitterness about the eventual outcome of their relationship, Freddy was adamant: 'Before we were married, her friends would pull me to one side and say, "Listen, don't take this the wrong way, but get out. She's a user. She's desperate to get into showbiz, and you're her ticket." I didn't believe them at the time, although she was very insecure.'

And seemingly these friends were right. The marriage lasted little more than three years and by then Demi had entered her wildest phase of parties, drink and drugs, running with the Hollywood crowd, edging perilously close to becoming a second-generation alcoholic. She confessed to using recreational drugs 'because I was young and not sure how to deal with my sudden burst of fame', and for many of those she partied with, it was the excitement of experimenting with the cocaine, LSD and Ecstasy cults which permeated 1980s America that drew them in.

She was also at this time enjoying her first taste of fame as a regular on the daytime soap *General Hospital* – the still-running drama series that had been on the air since the year after Demi arrived in the world. As you would expect, the storyline in each episode was pretty much predictable, as were the peripheral characters who drifted in and out. It was the story of the people and events surrounding the general hospital in Port Charles, a community on the coast of upper New York. Gloria Monty, who was the producer at the time, had been looking for someone to fill the part of Jackie Templeton, the sister of Laura (played by Janine Turner), who in a previous episode had disappeared into fog, and was now presumed dead. She thought Demi was perfect for the role. Strangely enough, however, Monty recalled, 'the network wasn't crazy about her. They didn't care for her voice, which I loved – it had a blues quality. But I was adamant about her [having the role]. She had such bravado. I remember she wore a rakish hat in rehearsal – a stetson she wore over one eye.'

According to Tony Geary (who played Luke Spender, the grieving husband, but who was now falling for his sister-in-law Jackie), 'Those were wild times. Demi was a lot of fun, but it was clear to people that the little box just wasn't going to hold her.'

Freddy Moore agrees. 'She started out on the fame trip when the producers wanted her to do talk-shows and media promotion,' he explains. 'They began flying her all over the place, and in the beginning I went too, since they were paying for first-class air tickets. She had tapped into a rich vein, and she didn't need me any longer. She was staying out later, till four and five in the morning, and turned into a totally different person.'

Later, Demi would shrug and admit, 'It [fame] gave me a certain kind of legitimacy.' Even though she would judge that, in *General Hospital*, she was still some way from her lucky break, her well-received performance in the series would, she hoped, at least bring her to the attention of Hollywood. How could it not? Her husky voice alone would have most falling at her feet. And, in retrospect, it is obvious that it was only a matter of time before someone would sign her up, even though she had no drama training to speak of. 'I never studied,' she confessed. 'I was too afraid to. I thought if an acting teacher had said to me, "You know what, you're no good," I wouldn't have gone any further. It was easier for me to justify going to an audition and getting rejected, maybe because they wanted somebody blonde, maybe because I wasn't experienced enough. I could live with that more easily.'

'But yes,' she elaborated, 'there was a part of me that felt that whenever I read anything [that required me to show] a depth of emotion I just had no idea how to act it. And then I started thinking maybe I didn't have to. Because in my personal life, I wasn't someone who cried easily, someone who was extremely vulnerable, you know, in the way that's constantly seeking out affirmation from other people. I've always been much more the person who took care of everyone else.'

It was a similar story as far as the notorious 'casting couch' was concerned. 'It definitely exists,' she said, 'but I can't say that I was ever harassed, at least not to the point where I think I've lost a job, or a role has been diminished because I didn't provide sexual favours for someone. There's maybe one encounter where I can remember someone encouraging me to undress to rehearse a scene . . . when I was young and much more vulnerable. But it exists everywhere, and Hollywood, obviously, is no exception. I just think Hollywood makes more colourful copy.'

In 1982 she landed the role of Patricia Wells in Charles Band's *Parasite*. It was a low-budget B-feature, just as her previous and mostly forgotten outings (in Garry Marshall's *Young Doctors in Love* and Silvio Narizzano's *Choices*) had been. *Parasite*, based on an original screenplay by Alan Alder and Frank Levering, 'with a dwindling cast of unknowns – young Demi prominent among them' (and even Freddy in a bit-part) – was, according to *Empire*, nothing more than a 'cheap rip-off of *Alien*'. To this day no movie has burst so violently into the popular consciousness than Ridley Scott's original 1979 shocker. For devotees and to most of the cinema-going public it still stands as one of the bench-marks of modern science fiction. And, from that point of view, it seemed almost pointless, even if in glorious 3-D, to revisit what was already a well-defined archetype.

Although the critics hated the film, Demi herself received some praise. Trevor Wallace, a British expatriate producer work-ing in Hollywood, remembers her clearly. 'She had the makings of a future actress of character even then. She had an alluring quality that directors and casting agencies look for. The voice was incredibly sexy. She had the type of appeal that could trans-late to the younger male audiences who, not to put too fine a point on it, judge their stars by bedroom imagery. But she was in a mess, emotionally and occasionally physically, and stuff like that gets around. At the time, she was carrying a good deal of baggage in that regard.'

Although anyone who saw *Parasite* forgot about it before their seats were even cold, Demi's performance was striking enough for producer Craig Baumgarten to add his seal of approval by offering her the lead – her first starring role – over Sally Field in director Jerry Schatzberg's 1984's *No Small Affair* in which she would play a struggling rock singer worshipped by Jon Cryer's character. Confirming Trevor Wallace's impression, Baumgarten knew 'from the very, very beginning she was going to be a movie star. I knew it when I saw the dailies. She can rip your heart out, make you care. That's a rare quality and part of what makes a star. When she was in pain, you just wanted to make her feel better.'

That same year she was cast as Michael Caine's daughter in one of the lesser roles of *Blame It on Rio*, Stanley Donen's much-hyped but, according to some, 'ultimately witless comedy'. Caine recalls Demi as being 'beautiful, young and a very skilled actress who impressed me so much that I can remember telling her that I thought she would be a star one day – and how right I was'. That particular movie did little to promote her cause, though. As Caine admits, it received a tremendous hammering in the press: 'I was stunned by the vehemence of the critics . . . but I'm glad to say the film went on to make a lot of money all over the world, despite the fuss.'

With her own finances now looking more healthy despite having only just quit the *General Hospital* set, Demi bought a house in Hollywood and asked her mother and her younger brother, Morgan, then fifteen, to move in. She equipped herself with a motorcycle and leathers and became a familiar figure racing, James Dean-style, up and down Sunset Boulevard. Things were looking good for the young actress; the only problem, as Virginia would later tell anyone who was prepared to buy her story, was that both mother and daughter were drinking heavily and getting more into drugs. After her school years of 'doing Quaaludes and smoking pot and drinking', her drug-taking at this point was becoming very serious. What she'd done in high school was, according to her, 'what the majority of the kids did', but she makes no bones about the impact it had on her life. The fact that the partying and wild times were now reaching a peak didn't really seem to matter to either daughter or mother – at least not then, anyway.

In fact, there had been several very close calls, professionally. One of those times occurred when director and screenwriter Joel Schumacher began to assemble the cast for his latest project, *St Elmo's Fire*. The actors in that film became the core of what the press later termed the 'Brat Pack', after the infamous earlier 'Rat Pack'. 'Our early life is a series of plateaux,' the director said at the time. 'Adulthood is a state that you're constantly defining for yourself as you go along, hoping that an adult is what other people will see.'

The early to mid-1980s saw the making of countless 'young adult' movies, but despite some remarkable box-office successes, the sad fact was most were flat and stereotypical. *St Elmo's Fire* was intended as an antidote to all of that. 'We wanted to dramatise the passion and uncertainty of that time, to make a point about self-created drama,' said Schumacher. 'When most of us look back on our twenties, we see that a lot of the incredible drama we went through was self-created. I hope that older people will be reminded of what they went through and younger people will see something of themselves and their own lives.'

*St Elmo's Fire* examined the way a group of friends faced decisions in real life that would determine their future. As far as producer Lauren Shuter was concerned, 'it confronts the problems of what happens to friendships after a life change, such as graduating from school, marriage, divorce or changing jobs.' The theme that lies at the heart of the movie was how going out in the world for the first time is a universal experience.

The principal roles were taken by Andrew McCarthy as an obituary writer who longs for better things, Judd Nelson as a philanderer who is having an affair with Ally Sheedy, Mare

Winningham as a virgin social worker enamoured with Rob Lowe, and Emilio Estevez as a law student and part-time waiter whose resurrected infatuation with former fellow student Andie MacDowell flowers into a compelling fixation.

In real life, of course, it would be Demi that Estevez fell for. From the moment they screen-tested together, he and Demi became an item. The affair lasted throughout the filming of the movie and for a couple of years after that. If nothing else, their relationship at least provided Hollywood with some new morsels of gossip.

Part of the Sheen acting dynasty that included, more famously, his father Martin and brother Charlie, Estevez was already carving out his own reputation in Hollywood with a career that was as promising as Demi's. A native New Yorker raised in California, he was born only a few months before her, on 12 May 1962, and had shared his father's love of movies ever since he had visited the set of Francis Ford Coppola's 1979 *Apocalypse Now* in the Philippines, and for one scene, cut from the final movie, even got a small bit-part. Not to be discouraged, he appeared the following year in *Seventeen Going Nowhere* before landing his breakthrough role, two years later, in *Tex*, and then featuring in *The Outsiders*, *Repo Man* and *The Breakfast Club*, all of which took his career to new heights. Formerly anonymous as the hell-raising son of Martin Sheen, suddenly he was the star of what were some of the most successful Brat Pack movies of early 1980s America.

Estevez wasn't the only young actor chasing fame and fortune. He soon found himself in competition with a hoard of others all fighting for the same top billing, Demi among them. Strangely enough, she had not even been called for an audition for *St*

*Elmo's Fire* when Schumacher spotted her. The incident has all
the qualities of the famous discovery stories of old Hollywood. 'I
was walking along the office corridor at Universal and saw this
incredible-looking girl coming towards me, like a young Arabian
racehorse,' he remembered. 'I told my assistant to follow her and
find out if she was an actress. She was, and he got the name of
her agent. Demi was wild and reckless and rode a motorcycle, I
recall, without a helmet.'

The agent, probably baffled by this sudden turn of events,
nevertheless arranged for Demi to go for a reading. Although she
was given the role of the glamorous and rich Jules, a young
banker addicted to cocaine, and a desperately unhappy member
of the college graduate ensemble (a part for which Schumacher
had interviewed more than five hundred actresses), when Demi
turned up for the wardrobe fitting, staggering and clearly intoxi-
cated, she nearly lost out. Schumacher summoned her to his
office and told her she looked a wreck and smelled like a
brewery. If she didn't clean up her act, he warned her, she would
be fired. For one thing, the insurance companies who covered
the cost of making every movie were particularly unhappy and
strict about substance-abusers on set. If Schumacher hadn't
believed that Demi was exactly right for the role, she would have
been out there and then. Later, during the period of rehearsals,
the director persuaded the producers and the studio to invite her
to enter an all-expenses-paid residential drug-treatment programme. She agreed and, as Schumacher puts it, 'within twenty-
four hours had turned herself around . . . [it was] an
extraordinarily mature step in a very fragile life'.

Although she probably couldn't forgive herself for almost
losing such an important role, neither did she forget the kindness

which Schumacher had shown her. According to one source, Joel had told her that he wasn't 'going to do what they did to John Belushi. I'm not going to give you this money so that you can kill yourself.' At that point, all he could envision 'was this gorgeous, talented girl dying on her motorcycle because she was so loaded'. But with counselling, and her later attendance at meetings of Adult Children of Alcoholics, Demi came out of her drug-fuelled days with her head clear, a young woman with positive goals which she proceeded to tick off in an almost clinical fashion.

New York-based writer Leslie Bennetts, who first met Demi soon after her appearance in *St Elmo's Fire*, said she reminded her of a female Gatsby. She had decided who she wanted to be and proceeded to make herself into that person. Schumacher would have agreed. Looking back, he said, 'I really admired her. I always remember the scene when Jules is committing suicide by freezing to death. She's sitting in the middle of an empty room with a big T-shirt on. Demi wanted to do the scene naked because she thought it would be more real. And I thought, for her to be that daring at that age . . . so, of course, I always smile when I see nude photos of her.'

Rob Lowe, an accomplished actor who would nevertheless become more famous for what he did for the benefit of his own private video cameras than for anything he accomplished on the silver screen, thought much the same. 'We were all on the set, trying to make sense of a multi-character piece. Demi had bigger fish to fry, worrying about "How do I get through this day alive and deliver any sort of performance?". I've never seen Demi anything other than aggressively professional on a movie set.' But yes, he admits, 'before rehab, absolutely, there was a lot of craziness'.

To this day, he remembers his first meeting with her very well, mainly because he didn't have a clue who the gorgeous young figure standing in front of him was. 'I'd never seen anything like it. Her hair was almost down to her butt and she had it pulled up and wrapped around the base of a straw hat. It was so bizarre – sort of like a hair hat.'

Filmed on location in the Washington DC metropolitan areas of historic Georgetown, the Adams-Morgan community, the Chesapeake and Ohio Canal, and the nearby University of Maryland fraternity row, *St Elmo's Fire* was released in July 1985 to a strangely bemused reaction from the critics. The movie was a let-down as far as they were concerned. The young audiences who flocked to it did not agree: for them, it was perfect – even if Demi wasn't crazy about her performance. 'In truth,' she said later, 'the perspective I have of myself in memory is that I was the least equipped and not as good as everyone else. They all seemed to have so much more confidence and assurance than I did.'

Demi was given precious little time to register any of the critics' reviews, however. After completing *St Elmo's Fire*, she journeyed to the set of her next movie, *One Crazy Summer*, in Massachusetts. Based on director Savage Steve Holland's own semi-autobiographical comedy, it was the story of teenager Hoops McCann (John Cusack) who wants to graduate from high school and become an artist. His parents, unfortunately, have other ideas. They hope he will earn himself a college athletic scholarship and achieve fame and fortune as a basketball star – despite the fact he can't even play the game or as much as slam-dunk into a wastepaper basket. The only thing Hoops yearns for is an education at the Rhode School of Design, where the entrance requirement is to write and illustrate a love story. The problem is that Hoops, by his own admission, knows little about that particular subject. He has never been in love. His best friend, George (Joel Murray), has the solution. He convinces Hoops to spend the summer holidays with him in Nantucket where they will, he promises, 'scale mermaids' and have a wonderful time and where he can find the inspiration for his college assignment. In fact he finds romance, adventure and a cornucopia of characters including Demi's Cassandra, a street-smart, sensitive beauty and the beacon who rescues him from his loveless slump and inspires him to write his love story and more.

Cassandra, however, has aspirations of her own. She has long wanted to make it as a singer and songwriter, but what with trying to save her grandfather's home and its elderly inhabitants from the unscrupulous land barons who intend to knock it down and replace it with housing developments and fast-food chains, she has to put those dreams aside.

And that was *One Crazy Summer*, a movie that, as *Empire* magazine put it, was 'a kooky, scattershot comedy that doesn't quite hang together. Although Demi turns in a credible performance and Cusack has a few hilarious moments, the plot doesn't really stand up, not even to the most cursory examination.'

That may be true, but Demi had no regrets about accepting the role. She even had the opportunity to indulge her singing voice on the soundtrack. 'Music has always been a passion for me,' she confessed later, 'but I never felt secure enough about my voice to present myself as a singer.' For two weeks, eight hours a day during pre-production, she worked with the film's songwriter Hawk Wolinski to choose her own musical material. 'It's great to realise I can do something I've only ever fantasised about.'

One of Holland's primary reasons for casting Demi was that

after their initial meeting, and without seeing any of her previous films or having her read for the part, 'she came in with this big husky voice, and was tough and really sure of herself, but also sensitive and goofy at times. It was a great blend of qualities for Cassandra.' The director had already sat through scores of other aspiring young singers and actresses looking for one who could do both. None could, or at least not like Demi. Her singing tape was submitted to Holland, and he realised there and then that his search had ended.

No sooner was her work completed on *One Crazy Summer* than she was starting work on yet another movie. Joining Rob Lowe, her ally from *St Elmo's Fire*, she headed for the set of *About Last Night* – the slick and cleaned-up version of David Mamet's play *Sexual Perversity in Chicago*.

Writing in the *Chicago Sun-Times* in July 1986, critic Roger Ebert offered one of the most astute summaries of the film: 'If one of the pleasures of movie-going is experiencing moments of recognition – times, when we can say, "Yes! That's exactly right, that's exactly the way it would have happened" – then this is a movie filled with moments like that. It has an eye and an ear for the way we live now, and it has a heart, too, and a sense of humour. It is one of the rarest of recent American movies, because it deals fearlessly with real people instead of with special effects.' More importantly, added Ebert, the film offers 'Lowe and Moore the best acting opportunities either one has ever had, and they make the most of them. Moore is especially impressive. There isn't a romantic note she isn't required to play in this movie, and she plays them all flawlessly.' Indeed, he continued to rave, '*About Last Night* is a warm-hearted and intelligent love story, and one of the year's best movies.'

The plot centred on Danny, a young salesman for a Chicago grocery wholesaler (played by Lowe), and Demi's character, Debbie, an art director for a Michigan Avenue advertising agency who, after meeting up at a soft-ball game in Grant Park, and then in the singles bars of Rush Street, begin to fall in love, and in the course of their year together, are seen trying to work out what that means to them.

With her work on *About Last Night* completed, Demi attended a series of press interviews alongside her co-stars. She sat on the edge of her chair with her hands folded in her lap, hesitating over every word as if she was afraid of saying something wrong. Her life was all about getting better, every day, in every way. Her determination to move forward was so relentless it was almost scary.

After the chaos and confusion of her early adult life, it was no wonder the young actress was seeking security. 'I have to move on,' she told journalist Leslie Bennetts at the time. 'I don't want to be in a problem. I want to be in a solution. I don't want to wallow. Where did I stash the grief? I processed it, little by little. I realised I could either be trapped by what was going on around me or I could find a way out.' She chose the way out.

What was interesting to observe as she struggled with her mental transformation was that her physical looks altered as well. She also seemed to have discovered the secret of a stable relationship with Emilio Estevez.

# FIRST LOVE

*'Emilio was definitely my first love'*
DEMI MOORE

When *Moviegoer* magazine caught up with Emilio Estevez in May 1986, Demi (whom *Time* magazine had just named as one of the six hottest actresses in Hollywood) was apologising for her boyfriend's late arrival. 'I forced him to go to a screening of my movie *About Last Night*,' she explained. Even when Estevez did turn up, it was in a burst of laughter and mild embarrassment. A lot of that he put down to the calendar notation he had scribbled for the midday interview with, as he and Demi put it, 'the *Moviegoer* dude.' Freshly sunburned and exchanging I-love-yous, the couple had just returned from 'a beautiful cruise down the Mexican Riviera' having finished shooting their second film together the previous month. *Wisdom* was the story of the title character, John Wisdom (Estevez), who is fuelled by the madcap high spirits of graduation night to steal a car. He is arrested and, with a criminal record, now has no possibility of making a career for himself in law or medicine as he had always planned. Suddenly forced to face a life that seems to have no future, he turns to crime. Armed with machine-gun, nervous bravado and girlfriend Demi, he sets out to rob banks by destroying mortgage and loan documents to save debt-ridden folks from the system's grasp. Heroes or hoods, the couple ride together cross-country in a Subaru wagon, eating junk-food, singing songs and making love.

For some time, the press would refer to Estevez's project as nothing more than an extravagant indulgence for the directional début of its writer and star – the youngest, incidentally, in Holly-wood history. It was scheduled for release in the late winter of 1986, to be followed in May 1987 by its international début at the Cannes Film Festival during 20th Century Fox's preview screenings of forthcoming attractions. At the time, he warned, the first cut of the movie wasn't quite right. The editing, music and narration – the things that make a movie sparkle – had not yet had their final polish. But, as far as the critics were concerned, it wouldn't be worth trying to make it any better. Some found the whole thing preposterous. One, the movie reviewer in *Variety*, prepared to make allowances for the fact that it was the actor's début as a director, nevertheless opined that it suffered from 'a completely implausible script and unending sophomoric dialogue'. Well aware of the movie's faults, Estevez would later probably agree with that summation. 'If I'm watching television now and the movie comes on, the first thing I do is change the channel to CNN,' he groaned.

As for Demi, 'she springs to life whenever she's given a good sarcastic line to deliver,' wrote Paul Attanasio in the *Washington*

*Post*. 'And if you stick around till the end, because your date wants to get his money's worth or whatever, there's a doozy of a car chase. If it had compromised the whole of *Wisdom*, it would have lifted the movie to artistic heights previously scaled by Sunday-afternoon stock-car racing on ABC's *Wide World of Sports*.'

Again, it was not high praise. Even worse for the couple was the fact that as they read yet another unsympathetic review of their on-screen romance, they also had to face the callous dissection of their off-stage love by the press. Demi and Emilio, of course, had been the subject of the tabloid gossip factory ever since they had gone public with their relationship the previous year. At that time, Demi's association with Estevez had, according to many of the journalists who quizzed her about her early life, ensured her position in the spotlight at a time when she was a relatively unknown actress. Although the couple would be together for almost three years, and the association with the scion of a modern acting dynasty provided something of a safe haven in a volatile Tinsel Town during the crucial and formative years of her career, the ubiquitous Hollywood insiders still found Demi's past of considerably greater interest.

She formally announced their engagement on a television chat-show in the winter of 1986, and talked of the elaborate plans she and Emilio had developed for a pre-Christmas wedding on 6 December that same year. The fact that she was still married to Freddy Moore didn't seem to have entered her head. Just weeks after the invitations had been sent out, however, the couple called the whole thing off – or, rather, Demi did. 'We were at two different junctures of our internal lives,' she explained dutifully at the time. 'There were things I needed, like security, that Emilio wasn't in a position to offer me.'

It was around this time that Emilio was summoned to his father's home to deal with what was described as a pressing family problem of a delicate nature. He was facing a $2 million paternity suit, and Martin Sheen wanted to know if the child in question was in fact Emilio's, and, if so, what he intended to do about it. Above all else, he was told that he should deal with the situation responsibly – any new member of the Sheen family could not be ignored. When he returned, Demi, true to her resolve, broke up with him. Within no time at all, the tabloid press got hold of the story and were reporting that the two young movie stars had called it quits. Although they weren't dating any more, they remained very close friends.

(Later, interestingly enough, Estevez, who at the time publicly denied the palimony and child-support claim by model Carey Salley had, according to court records, been paying Salley $3,000 a month, while his father, Martin – adhering to his promise – arranged for the child's baptism, and provided extra financial support for his grandchild's mother.)

The press, meanwhile, were quick to notice that Demi did not remain alone for long. In July 1987, just a few months after breaking up with Estevez, a mutual friend introduced her to Bruce Willis, the wisecracking gumshoe hero of the very popular television series *Moonlighting*, who was in town for the screening of Estevez's new movie, *Stakeout*. It was here, according to some, that Bruce and Demi began their intense relationship. At first, though, it seems she was not at all impressed, showing little interest in the much-headlined hell-raiser who had just a few weeks previously emerged from the police cells following his arrest for boisterous behaviour. Her disinterest may have been due to the fact that she saw in Willis's behaviour too much of her own past – and from which she was now making a timely and exacting recovery in order to save her own career from crashing almost before it began. The fact that she had already experienced the pitfalls, and had survived most of them pretty much unscathed, was for her of crucial importance. Her arrival in his life came at a point when he, too, was forced to make a dramatic turnaround in his own attitudes and social behaviour.

Although Demi had a decidedly overblown reputation as a recovering wild child – due in part to leaks from publicists on the movies she had worked on, and also thanks to the close attachment she had had with the bad-boy Sheen dynasty – she certainly wasn't a world-famous movie star yet. Neither for that matter was Willis. He was nevertheless captivated by her beauty and was intrigued by the off-hand manner with which she deflected his flirtatious advances. This was something he was not used to.

Walter Bruce Willis (or Bruno as he is often called) was born in Idar-Oberstein in Germany, and raised in Penns Grove, New Jersey, one of four children of David and Marlene Willis. After graduating from high school and flitting between truck driving and night security work at a couple of factory plants, he attended drama at Montclair State College. After that he headed out to New York to audition for some off-Broadway stage productions, making ends meet by bartending at Kamikaze and Café Central. He landed his first role in Sam Shepherd's 1984 film *Fool for Love*, which brought him to the attention of Triad Artists (the same agency, incidentally, that one year later would sign twelve-year-old Winona Horowitz, later Ryder, to their books, long before she had done any professional work). Soon after, Bruce found himself auditioning in Los Angeles for Stanley Kubrick's *Full Metal Jacket* and, with three thousand other hopefuls, for the role of David Addison in a television series named *Moonlighting*. Loosely based around a private detective agency, the programme starred Cybill Shepherd, who was perhaps best known at the time for her role as Betsy in Martin Scorsese's *Taxi Driver* and her off-screen relationships with Peter Bogdanovich and Elvis Presley during the same period.

Like so many other hopeful actors, Willis was where Demi had been a few years earlier – though in terms of getting attention, he was doing it through a megaphone. The word around Hollywood was still that he was just another television big-timer who would never make it on to the silver screen – despite the fact that he had just completed his first starring role in director Blake Edwards' *Blind Date* alongside Kim Basinger.

Almost before she knew what was happening, Demi was firmly and resolutely in his life, and during that summer of 1987, when Willis had so much going for him yet was in danger of scuttling his own raft of success, the first delicate beginnings of what would soon be headlined as the romance of the decade took hold.

In October of that year, Willis went teetotal, took counselling and attended Alcoholics Anonymous sessions at the Cedars Sinai Medical Center in Los Angeles. On top of that, more importantly, he now had the support of Demi who, of course, knew very well what it felt like to give up the demon drink. The gossip-columnists would later claim Bruce gave up the booze for her and that she had given him an ultimatum stating 'either quit drinking or we're through', and although it was never quite as simple as that, Demi did encourage and help him through most of it. They both knew from experience that the dizzy oblivion of drugs or passing out in a drunken stupor was no solution to whatever problem they were facing.

It probably didn't help the delicate situation that the previous month the couple had gone public with their relationship when they turned up arm in arm and clearly in love at the Emmy awards. The tabloid press were cruelly dismissive, still convinced that Demi was just the latest in the long line of women who had been involved with Willis. It would never last, they claimed, and they certainly didn't believe that she might have tamed 'the wild bad boy of Hollywood'.

Within a few weeks, however, a string of blurry snapshots of Bruce and Demi romping in the surf at Malibu, taken through a paparazzo's long-sighted lens from about a quarter of a mile away promptly silenced the doubters. It seemed the couple were now heading towards a full-blown romance, the tabloid press conceded, but no one was talking about a wedding, they insisted.

But then, on 21 November 1987, the couple surprised everyone, including close friends and especially Demi's mother. They flew off to Las Vegas, ostensibly to see Julio Cesar Chavez win the light-heavyweight boxing crown from Edwin Rosario. That night, apparently on impulse, they registered with the Clerk County Marriage Bureau in Las Vegas, and just before midnight a Justice of the Peace, probably Charlotte Richards, arrived at their room at the Golden Nugget Hotel to marry them. (Other sources suggested they were married in the famous Little White Chapel where, among others, Frank Sinatra, Judy Garland and Mickey Rooney had declared their vows. One of five owned by Richards along the Vegas Strip, it was then, and probably still is today, the most famous of the hundred other chapels that specialise in what has become one of the city's most enduring traditions – the quickie wedding.)

Hotel room or chapel, it didn't really matter. News of the

wedding soon hit the wires and the press pack descended upon Las Vegas to inspect the records. Once there, they discovered that Demi had declared herself a spinster, omitting to state that she had previously been married. An anonymous telephone call stirring up trouble, or a tabloid headline, sent the police in to investigate the caller's hint of a bigamous marriage and claims that the new Mrs Willis was not officially divorced from Freddy Moore.

It was untrue, of course, although the press had a field day with the 'shock horror' news that she had failed to mention her previous marriage, and even produced photocopies of her marriage certificate to prove it. It was blown out of all proportion and mattered not at all in the end except to feed the gossip-columnists and the appetites of readers of the scandal sheets who more or less disregarded Demi's explanation that she did not have the documents at hand to prove that she was divorced. She had feared it may delay the marriage.

The story wouldn't disappear, though, and the situation only worsened when, during a television interview some time later, she announced that Bruce Willis was her first husband, and she now had the wedding licence to prove it. When Freddy Moore heard that, his response was disbelieving: 'She's probably very embarrassed that she made a mistake,' he laughed. 'It's interesting that she lied – perhaps she never told Bruce about me.' The press were even more intrigued later, when Freddy told them she had also lied about her age when the two of them had got married. At the time, she said she was twenty-one when in truth she was really only sixteen.

Three weeks later, Demi and Bruce celebrated that quiet Las Vegas wedding with a spectacular bash more in keeping with their status as the new and fascinating focus of Hollywood matrimony. They hired a studio sound stage for a second ceremony, specially chosen so that the media helicopters could not zoom in low and capture the action on film. They invited 450 guests. Demi, looking as beautiful as ever, wore a $10,000 wedding gown, and was given a $60,000 Mercedes as a wedding present from Bruce. They wrote their marriage vows together for the ceremony, and spoke the words clearly and precisely, declaring their undying love, looking into each other's eyes: 'I do, I do.' They were, they insisted, simply a young couple very much in love.

Willis even wrote a song for the occasion, 'Bruno's Getting Married', which a dozen of his best friends sang as the wedding party came up the aisle with their twelve ushers and twelve bridesmaids, one of whom was Ally Sheedy, Demi's co-star from *St Elmo's Fire*. Not that she was surprised. As she later told US magazine 'the quickest route to power for an actress in Hollywood is to hook yourself up with someone who can put you in a good position and make yourself into a sex object.' The '50s rock star Little Richard, now an ordained minister, conducted the service to the accompaniment of the thirty-strong gospel choir, before returning to his rock'n'roll persona for the wedding breakfast that followed. With a platoon of security guards providing a veritable ring of steel round the festivities, the paparazzi couldn't get within a mile of the place.

As they had done to so many others before them, the tabloids hounded the couple from the moment their relationship went public, and although the two actors did their best to shrug off the attention, they had little defence against the constant hurtful, insidious nagging that quickly drove them both crazy. The first few months of their married life together were spent apart on movie sets. While Willis filmed John McTernan's *Die Hard*, Demi was taking part in *The Seventh Sign*, directed by Carl Schultz. Although their schedules meant an aching separation for both, work would nonetheless provide a welcome respite from the daily harassment of the popular press. Indeed, it would be several months before the couple were again seen out in public. On New Year's Eve they turned up for a party at Spago's restaurant on Sunset Boulevard with seven bodyguards – a situation which, according to the Hollywood grapevine, was now part and parcel of their fame. For the scandal-sheet hacks, of course, it was perfect: anything that looked like excess and self-importance on the part of the couple was simply perfect material for them. The image created by the seven bodyguards was, however, a total distortion, complained Willis: one was hired to protect Demi and the rest were employees of the restaurant who were simply helping them through the crush of photographers waiting outside.

It was much the same, if not worse, a few weeks later when they attended a screening in Los Angeles of the remake of Roger Vadim's famous *And God Created Woman*, with Rebecca de Mornay in the Brigitte Bardot role. Arriving outside the cinema slightly later than planned, they were immediately surrounded by Hollywood's ravenous paparazzi. As they dashed into the foyer, pursued by the crowd of hacks, Demi, four months pregnant, stumbled and fell. Even then, there was no let up. Willis, losing his temper, exploded in frustration. 'Get the fuck outta here! That's enough!' he screamed, pushing the photographers aside, his face contorted with rage, and yelling again, 'Leave us the fuck alone!' And that was the picture they got. It appeared in just about all the papers the next day. And it was also the photograph that would come out time and time again whenever he was in the media doghouse.

With the completion of *Die Hard*, Bruce Willis had, in the eyes of the press, performed the showbusiness equivalent of winning the lottery or hitting the jackpot on a Las Vegas slot machine. To them, he was public property and so was his wife and the rest of his life. But did the world really need to know about the couple's private business? And did we have to see it splashed on the front of every tabloid? The announcement that they were expecting their first child together that summer was not enough to silence the rumours of imminent disaster that had haunted Hollywood since minutes after their wedding: they were breaking up, they had broken up, it was drugs, it was an affair, it was a host of other things.

Demi, meanwhile, was none too pleased at constantly being defined as 'the new wife of Bruce Willis', rather than being recognised as an actress herself. Wherever she went and whoever she spoke to, whatever newspaper or magazine article she picked up, the references were always the same, and especially now that she was expecting his baby. Nonetheless, it was something that raised her profile. Even though she had spouted the words so many times before, perhaps it took her until now to realise that she really didn't need that kind of visibility. The question was, if she didn't want that, what did she want?

For a considerable period, whenever she did interviews, the first question was invariably: 'What's it like being married to Bruce Willis?' or 'How come you managed to tame Hollywood's bad boy?' The more daring even may have asked, 'Is is true your marriage is in trouble?' In the end, she simply refused to discuss her husband, and he did likewise when questioned about her. They rejected all attempts to get them together to be photographed as Hollywood's hottest couple. It was simply out of the question and strictly off-limits.

Demi's new film, about to hit the screens that spring, was the apocalyptic thriller *The Seventh Sign* in which, in keeping with her own life, she played the role of a pregnant woman. As far as the movie publicists were concerned, they couldn't have asked for better timing. They could perhaps have done without Demi's resolve to establish her own identity, though.

While she was promoting *The Seventh Sign* and starting to see that, in pushing her own cause and her own work, having a more famous partner did have its benefits, she was nevertheless determined to rise above the Bruce Willis syndrome. That fact alone would cause more friction among their respective handlers, and between themselves, than anything else. 'I am Demi Moore, not Mrs Bruce Willis,' she repeated countless times. For some, it was evidence that the marriage was already in trouble, when in fact all she was doing was making it clear from the outset that she was going forward as herself and not just as her husband's wife.

With this in mind, her new movie was bound to attract attention. Critic Roger Ebert said it was the kind of film he enjoyed most – thrillers about biblical prophecies, the Second Coming and the Antichrist. 'After the sheer anarchy unleashed upon Hollywood by the slice-and-dice movies, it's actually comforting to know the characters in this film play by the rules,' he wrote. 'They believe in good and evil, and they act as if individual human beings can have an influence on the outcome of events. Compared to the *Friday the 13th* world view, *The Seventh Sign* is positively sanguine.'

Demi played Abby Quinn, a neurotic young woman who has had a miscarriage and now, pregnant again, is fearful of losing another baby. The story begins in the last two months of her pregnancy when, with her husband Russell (played by Michael

Biehn) lending moral support, she becomes convinced that her unborn child will play an important role in the chain of events that signals the end of the world, a time when rivers will run with blood, the seas will boil, the desert freeze, the birds fall from the sky and the earth will shake. Her fears are, of course, borne out of the discovery that the strange man with burning eyes who has just rented the small apartment over the garage in her backyard possesses ancient Hebrew manuscripts in unidentifiable code.

Whatever else, Ebert continued, 'Moore is strong and clear in the movie's central role, and proves once again, after *About Last Night*, that she has genuine charisma, an aura of intelligence and resolve, reinforced by her throaty voice. I was not sure at first, however, that she was the correct choice for this movie. I thought she was perhaps too strong, and that the role required more of a screamer. Not so. By the end of the film, she is called upon to save the planet and all living things upon it, and so she needs that strength. She provides a strong centre to the film, but the rest of it, alas, is all over the map.'

That is a fair judgement. At the same time, though, Demi's performance was enough to save the film from being trashed by the critics. Although the movie itself was generally dismissed, she at least won recognition. If nothing else, *The Seventh Sign* was probably the first film which let her display her true talent. Her part in it is a role she can be proud of and can be seen as the culmination of every conviction and strength she had played in other roles in the past. From now on, there would be no stopping the very determined and exceedingly ambitious Demi Moore.

Interestingly enough, it was only at this point, when she was actively seeking the limelight of publicity – for the specific reason of promoting her film – and Willis was positively

shunning it, that a subtle change was noticeable in their relationship, producing some interesting side elements that
perhaps neither had really discussed or considered in detail
before they married. Demi, clearly now on the road to stardom,
still needed a hook on which to hang her coat, and for all young
actors that traditionally meant succumbing to a series of interviews to boost their current movie. In spite of her earlier
protestations about maintaining her own identity, Demi now
found it virtually impossible in those days to discuss her work
without reference to her husband.

As a couple, they were fascinatingly attractive and represented
a rare combination in Hollywood. In spite of the open derision
they faced from some sections of their profession, the headline-
grabbing qualities of their lives – past, present and future –
offered intriguing talking points. Indeed, there were very few
couples in Hollywood where both husband and wife were such
high-profile figures and, as such, they offered all kinds of pos-
sibilities for insight and speculation. Although Demi herself was
still some way from being an A-list star, she was nevertheless
building a solid reputation as an actress and commanded close
attention for her relationship with Willis. This situation intensified, of course, with confirmation that she was pregnant and that
Willis, Hollywood's bad boy, was to become a father.

Although their marriage, the forthcoming birth and their
movies prompted a fresh deluge of stories about every aspect of
their lives imaginable, Demi, unlike Bruce, still co-operated with
the media when it was a question of her work. Even as she
awaited the release of *The Seventh Sign*, she gave a frank interview to *Vanity Fair* about her aspirations and was photographed
on the beach at Malibu and inside their home. Such attention, at

that stage of her career, was very welcome, and was seen as a necessary part of her bid for stardom in the movies – and exactly what Willis had been able to avoid through his instant fame from television. By now, mega-stardom was undoubtedly close at hand, but she needed to achieve it on her own terms. Bruce had to adapt to that determination just as she had to accept his desire for no publicity.

Although jealous rivals suggested that it was simply by being associated with Bruce Willis that a host of opportunities had opened up for her and ultimately furthered her career, Demi rejected these accusations – they simply weren't true.

The fact that she was now heavily pregnant worked out as a blessing for the couple. It enabled her to climb off the Hollywood merry-go-round for a while and concentrate on nothing more than the forthcoming birth. It would in fact be eighteen months before she accepted another movie role. Bruce, too, was still tied to his *Moonlighting* television contract and would have found it difficult, if not impossible, to get involved in the making of many films at that time.

As Demi reached the final stages of her pregnancy, they calculated the baby could be expected while Willis was in Kentucky on the set of his next film, *In Country*, with Emily Lloyd (the British actress known at that time for her début role in *Wish You Were Here* but precious little else). It seemed only natural that they would arrange to have the baby born near by, despite the fact that Demi would not have the close medical supervision she would have received in Los Angeles.

Renting a country farmhouse in Kentucky not far from the set, Demi, surrounded by bodyguards and a battery of security systems powerful enough to protect a small city, arrived about three weeks before the baby was due, and immediately checked in with the local doctor. She had a list of things she wanted – and things she didn't: 'I had a very clear idea of how I wanted the birth to be.' One of those things, as she put it, was to feel the whole experience of her body opening up to allow a human being to pass through, and to do that she opted for no drugs or pain relief, but she did want the whole thing videotaped.

With everything ready, it was just a question of waiting. One evening shortly afterwards, out with her husband at the pictures, Demi went into labour in the middle of the film. With a minimum of fuss, they returned home. She packed and prepared the personal items she thought she might need while Bruce phoned his film crew and the friends they'd asked to attend the birth. Soon after, arriving at the hospital, the guests who would witness the event gathered during the fifteen hours that Demi was in labour. Willis never left her side.

With three cameras set up at different angles, everything was in place to record the delivery. Among those watching were her massage therapist, her personal assistant, Bruce's best friend and aide, Demi's girlfriend and the video operator. Even when the time came, and the baby's head started to appear, Demi persevered to make sure it was all being captured on tape. It was. Willis, in the meantime, decked out in medical white robes and mask was, according to his wife, absolutely remarkable. Even though the doctor was present throughout, it was Bruce, Demi recalls, whose hands were inside her, pulling the baby out. 'I stayed very calm. It was never crazy. When she came slithering out, Bruce and the doctor cleared her mouth and Bruce put her on my chest. Then everyone left us alone for half an hour. We have it all on film, and we've watched it over and over again with our friends.'

Everything had gone according to plan. The child, a girl they named Rumer Glenn Willis, after the author Rumer Godden, was born on 16 August 1988.

# TABLOID
# HEAVEN

4

*'Everyone has their turn. They're nice to me, they're
shitty to me, they're nice to me, they're shitty to me.
And that's just the nature of it and I accept that'*
DEMI MOORE

By the time the new mother was preparing for her return to
work, she found herself once again in demand. Every offer she
received, however, now needed to be balanced against not just
what it would mean in terms of her film career and her efforts to
produce her own movies, but against the impact that accepting
would have on life with her new baby. Was it worth asking young
Rumer and her nanny to make the long, arduous commute from
Idaho to Los Angeles with her? From that point of view alone, it
was understandable if she became very discerning, only choosing
roles that justified the considerable upset to her new family life.

Without specifying which offers she turned down, she made it
plain that none of her decisions could be attributed to the fact

that she happened to be married to Bruce Willis. 'That has nothing to do with it,' she insisted. The only possible connection her next project had with Willis was that it featured Sean Penn, who was friends with Bruce.

Penn's career was, at that time, pretty much in the doldrums, and had been for some years. Despite his acting skills, he had been turned down for many roles of note – his own hell-raiser tag and a couple of police busts had done his reputation more harm than Willis's similar escapades had. Now, however, another of his good friends, Robert DeNiro, in the throes of setting up his own production company, TriBeca Films, had stepped in to launch a rescue operation. He promised Penn he would find a movie on which they could both work together. DeNiro persevered and finally came up trumps that summer of 1988. Art Linson, the producer of *The Untouchables* (which had brought so much praise for Sean Connery and Kevin Costner, and in which DeNiro himself had played a cameo as Al Capone), liked the idea of DeNiro and Penn working alongside each other. 'The prospect was very exciting to me,' he remembered. 'I suggested that the roles of convicts on the run could provide a good vehicle for them.' From that moment, Linson came up with the notion of filming a remake of *We're No Angels*, the 1955 black comedy which had starred Humphrey Bogart, Peter Ustinov and Aldo Ray.

Linson's first choice of screenwriter was Demi's old ally from *About Last Night*, David Mamet, who had scripted *The Untouchables* and Paul Newman's 1982 film *The Verdict* (in which Willis, incidentally, had appeared as an uncredited extra). Mamet was initially reluctant to take on the project, but agreed to produce a first-draft script based on the original. Linson was adamant that it wasn't a straight remake of the 1955 film: 'It's a movie very loosely based on some of the ideas in that film.'

All the same, attempting to find a new angle was difficult. In Mamet's screenplay, DeNiro and Penn, in the roles of Ned and Jim respectively, are a couple of small-time hoods sentenced to hard labour. After being forced to participate in a prison breakout, the two convicts, now on the run, take refuge in a New England town famous for a miraculous local shrine. In need of a miracle themselves to dodge the warden, sheriff, deputies and other officers of the law intent on recapturing them, dead or alive, they pose as a pair of priests, Father Reilly and Father Brown, who claim to have got lost on their way to the local monastery. The problem facing Ned and Jim is to maintain their disguises long enough to find a way to cross the nearby Canadian border on the outskirts of town – and before the real priests turn up. Their situation is further complicated by Ned's feelings towards Molly, played by Demi, a hot-tempered single mother who has a few unanswered prayers of her own.

The movie opened to fair reviews in December 1989, and although it figured well in the seasonal listings, it could not be considered a major hit in terms of either box-office receipts or its overall impact. Demi's own performance, however, was as strong as ever, even if it was, as some said, in a role that was neither major nor well defined. She appeared in only a few scenes and in most cases her character seemed almost an afterthought. The critics nonetheless rallied to her support. Roger Ebert was particularly encouraging: 'Demi Moore has a supporting role as a local woman with a child, but because no comic spin was put on her character, her scenes don't add much. They provide, in fact, a serious undercurrent that the movie doesn't necessarily need.'

As for DeNiro and Penn, Ebert continued, 'they are both essentially serious dramatic actors and maybe the reality of the location – where the small town of Mission in British Columbia was dressed up to match the Depression era – gave them such a solid grounding that they felt they had permission to act up the necessary goofiness.'

DeNiro adored the role he played. 'I liked the character of Ned,' he later told journalists. 'He and Jim share a cynical attitude about life until they experience, through a series of accidents, some quasi-miraculous events.'

Director Neil Jordan agreed. 'One of the things David Mamet did so well in his screenplay was to show how accidental events can fall into place in a way that makes them resemble acts of some higher power. Is it coincidence or a miracle? Mamet lets you draw your own conclusions.'

The director and production team went to extraordinary lengths to ensure the film was realistic in all aspects. Under the watchful eye of designer Wolf Kroeger, every object on the set was researched and selected for its authenticity. On location in the vicinity of Stave Lake Falls in British Columbia's Fraser Valley, east of Vancouver, where shooting commenced in late November 1988, the film-makers constructed the largest set ever built in Canada.

Demi, with third billing and a fee of less than $300,000, nevertheless came out of the deal well. After being tipped off by Sean Penn, she fought tooth and nail for the part. Once in, she justified her selection with a critically acclaimed performance in a relatively modest role. And that more or less summed up her position at the time.

Enjoying the freedom of being between movies, Demi continued reading new scripts as they came in, aware of what she was looking for and able to tell at a glance whether or not a particular idea was suitable. The role of Molly Jensen in Jerry Zucker's *Ghost* alongside Patrick Swayze and Whoopi Goldberg (already cast) was one she was very keen on. In fact, she had already told her agent at the Creative Artists Agency that she wanted the part.

Costing less than $15 million in production, the movie was released in America in July 1990 almost unnoticed, going into cinemas one week after Bruce Willis's first *Die Hard* sequel and in the wake of other bigger movies released that summer. Although the film was promptly dismissed by the critics as being nothing more than pleasant but rather soppy entertainment with engaging performances from the three principals, critic Roger Ebert remained upbeat about the film. He called *Ghost* 'a nice mixture of horror and humour, especially in the scenes involving Goldberg and her sisters'.

Other critics were more concerned about the film's fundamentalist view of heaven and hell. These were clearly depicted and the souls of the good and evil characters had been gathered up and directed to their assigned destinations in the afterlife. There were even debates in the media about the inner motives of revenge, a theme of the film, being good for the soul.

Good or bad, it seemed doubtful whether director Jerry Zucker and writer Bruce Joel Rubin ever intended any serious undertones. The movie was, in their view, an amiable and sentimental piece of frippery that just happened to catch the imagination of the cinema-going public, ever eager for answers to the eternal question.

*Ghost* certainly wasted no time in introducing that issue. Sam Wheat (Patrick Swayze), an investment broker, and Demi's character, Molly Jensen, a pottery sculptor, are in love and have never been happier than they are now, living together in their new loft apartment. Tragedy strikes quickly when Sam is murdered, apparently by a mugger, on a New York street as they return home after a night out. While Molly is left to grieve for Sam, he himself is beginning an uncanny new existence. Unbeknownst to her, he hangs around in spirit form to protect her and to relay the important information he has now discovered – that he was in fact killed by his 'friend' and crooked business associate, Carl Bruner (played by Tony Goldwyn). As well as that, he also needs to tell Molly how much he loves her, something he never did while he was alive.

Unable to affect anything in the physical world, and desperate to contact Molly whose own life is now under threat, Sam searches for a psychic to act as his voice. Eventually he comes across Oda Mae Brown (Whoopi Goldberg), a previously fraudulent séance practitioner who is shocked to discover that she does indeed possess the power to communicate with the spirit world – or at least with one particular ghost. Sam eventually persuades her to contact Molly with the usual 'only you will know this' information, but it takes a long, long time for the penny to drop. In the meantime, the still mourning Molly sides with the villain of the piece instead. Eventually, of course, she sees the error of her ways when Sam, in one of the finest moments of the movie, takes over Oda Mae's body to convince Molly she is the authentic medium she claims to be.

Discussing the movie's afterlife content, particularly the final scene, Demi said, 'I think when we've lost someone we all feel the desire for them to be back. Molly is given that opportunity to experience a last goodbye from Sam and be reassured that where he's going is a place of love.'

Jerry Zucker, the director, agreed. That was the element that fascinated him most when he first read Bruce Joel Rubin's screenplay. 'It was unlike anything I had read before – a thriller and a love story set in two worlds, the physical and the spiritual. It was a fantasy, but you couldn't help think that maybe that's the way it really is.'

All the same, it was all good clean fun, and Whoopi Goldberg – in need of a hit after being adrift too long on poor material – provided the roustabout humour essential to the story. 'There is a part of me that has always wanted to be a hero and Oda Mae permits me to play someone who becomes truly heroic,' she said. 'She has been making a bizarre living as a psychic. She's a scam artist who has been arrested many times. But when Sam as a ghost comes to her, it freaks her out. He needs her help.'

Within a few weeks of opening, *Ghost* had smashed into the box-office listings and assumed the proportions of a Hollywood miracle by eventually overtaking *Die Hard 2* and some of the other blockbuster movies of that summer. From there, *Ghost*-fever swept across the country and, by August 1990, the movie's US gross alone was $217 million. That figure, some said, was considerably more than Willis's film had achieved, and it was a record that was recognised at the 1991 Academy Awards cere-mony when *Ghost* was nominated in four categories: Best Supporting Actress for Goldberg, Best Original Script for Rubin, Best Picture and Best Editing. It walked away with two of them, for Goldberg and Rubin. More importantly, a couple of months previously, it had earned Demi her first-ever Golden Globe nomination, for Best Actress. A clear favourite in many people's eyes, she lost out to Julia Roberts in *Pretty Woman*.

With an eventual $450 million worldwide gross and the biggest-earning film of its kind, there was no doubt that Demi Moore was now a very important figure in Hollywood.

Although her part in *Ghost* was a role she could be proud of, it was nevertheless Swayze's and Goldberg's picture. That didn't matter much – as far as Demi was concerned, she was just as much the star as they were. She did, however, object that her character was not strong enough – she wasn't attracted to soft characters – and felt that Molly should have been less passive and more assertive. She fought Jerry Zucker all the way to the cutting-room. Although Demi lost the battle to get her own way, the director did admit that *Ghost* was a 'much better film for her input, as difficult as it was sometimes to hear.' After all the pushing and shoving that went on in production, it was something he couldn't even 'stand to admit'. Well, according to *Premiere* magazine, it wasn't.

Strangely enough, the one thing Zucker was at a loss to explain was why the actress was self-conscious about her smile on screen. 'I loved her smile,' he insisted. 'There was a scene where it was so wonderful but so brief. I don't think I ever told her, but I actually shot in slow motion, to prolong more of a smile. She was standing still long enough that it doesn't show up as slow-mo on screen.' In another interview later, he continued: 'Demi is seductive, and I don't just mean sexually. She has such an alluring manner – when she wants to draw you in, she can do it easily.'

Basking in the warm glow of her most successful movie yet, Demi now slipped easily into position among the top ten box-office stars. For all the limitations of her role, she had finally reached the place she wanted to be, but she'd done so not by playing the aggressive role she most probably would have preferred, but through the part of a rather lame character with cropped hair, elfin looks and doe eyes. Still, that didn't stop her seizing every opportunity to make her demands heard, both during the filming and, insistently louder, as the film's release drew closer. 'She learned from a master demander,' said one unnamed studio executive talking to *The Guardian*. 'Only, unlike Bruce, she didn't earn it. Demi has always been impatient while waiting for things to come to her. She says she doesn't ride on her husband's coattails, but when she hired a bodyguard after *Ghost*, that was fame by association.'

By the time she arrived in France for the European press and promotional junkets for the film, she was, according to journalist Jennet Conant, 'in the throes of a fully fledged star trip'. She would travel only by private aircraft, and she was being attended by an assistant who had an assistant, along with three other people who did her hair, make-up and wardrobe, plus a masseuse. 'Of all the female stars in France that week promoting movies, including Whoopi Goldberg and Goldie Hawn, Demi was the only one who felt the need of a bodyguard.'

It was that particular aspect of her claim to fame that annoyed the press more than any other. And what really threatened to cause grief among the local media was her insistence that she should have pre-publication approval of any photograph taken of her. 'Who the fuck does she think she is?' complained one journalist. 'Nobody asks for photo approval, not even Princess Diana.'

It took several weeks and some crucial discussions with

worried studio executives before Demi agreed to drop this demand, but she wasn't happy and, if anything, the incident cemented her determination.

It was a similar story when she was promoting *Indecent Proposal* in Britain a couple of years later. Studio executives were embarrassed and on edge as she told the sixty Fleet Street veterans gathered to attend her press conference that she would only pose for approved photographers. She could not allow herself to be the 'object of someone else's choice. That doesn't seem right, because this is about *me*. I must retain control of what image of me is published. It is essential.' She continued to work from then on with that same sense of determination in mind whenever she set about promoting future movies.

But after a few mutterings from the press, roughly translating as 'get lost', she was once again forced to withdraw her demands, and with great reluctance she agreed to pose for one or two photographs – but 'only the serious newspapers – no tabloids'.

In the wake of the success of *Die Hard 2* and *Ghost* both films had a remarkable effect on the standing of Bruce Willis and Demi Moore. One can only imagine the millions of dollars that poured into their household from those two films alone. Just as Willis had become a sensation virtually overnight, Demi was now matching his rise to stardom. They were now a successful double act and as such became the focus of renewed attention as the most talked-about, most written-about, most admired and most hated couple in Hollywood.

Comparisons, of course, were made to all the previous and current Hollywood pairings. Successful couples were and still are farirly thin on the ground. Clark Gable and Carole Lombard, Spencer Tracy and Katherine Hepburn, Humphrey Bogart and

Lauren Bacall, Paul Newman and Joanne Woodward, Elizabeth Taylor and Richard Burton, Robert Wagner and Natalie Wood, Kurt Russell and Goldie Hawn, Tom Cruise and Nicole Kidman, Johnny Depp and Winona Ryder, Kiefer Sutherland and Julia Roberts were among the biggest-name relationships, but none of them could claim to wield the kind of power that Bruce Willis and Demi Moore did. Suddenly they were 'Hollywood's Hottest Couple' more than any other.

As they had done to a thousand famous faces before them, though, the press, who had built up Demi and Bruce into super-stars, just had to bring them back down to earth. They were sitting ducks in the hothouse atmosphere of Tinsel Town. Fuelled by comments from jealous or spiteful rivals, who branded them a pair of prima donnas with so little pedigree that they might be called movie mongrels, the tabloid gossips went into overdrive. The sniping that began then, during that hot Los Angeles summer, would build into a vicious stream of vitriol to which would be added the voice of Demi's tell-all mother, Virginia.

As soon as Demi hit the big time in *Ghost*, the tabloids began tearing into her past and soon uncovered the details of Virginia's drink problems and Demi's wild-child days and nights. A posse of scandal scribes, chequebooks in hand, tracked down Virginia, now a recovering alcoholic who still fell off the wagon every now and then. She had recently had several brushes with the law from which her daughter had bailed her out on a couple of occasions. Now, realising how valuable her inside knowledge of Holly-wood's latest star could be, she was ready to tell all – for the right price, of course.

Beneath one headline – 'MUM JOINED DEMI IN DRUGS PARTY: *GHOST* BEAUTY'S COCAINE SHAME' – ran the story of how 'Demi Moore went on a wild drink and drugs binge with her mother'. Virginia spared no detail: 'Life was one long sick party,' she said. It looked like she was using her daughter's fame as her own ticket to ride. She had received several large cash donations from Demi – some reports said as much as $45,000 in staged payments – to aid her recovery from alcoholism. Unlike her daughter, though, Virginia couldn't get straight. On one occasion she was arrested for drink-driving in New Mexico and spent three days in jail. Demi refused to bail her out this time because she hoped being behind bars would help shock her mother into cleaning up her act. It didn't.

America's sleaziest tabloids targeted Virginia and gathered up the more lurid aspects of Demi's past, even though the actress herself had been quite open about her history. A string of salacious stories filled the gossip columns for months on end as Demi now became a serious contender among the select band of top actresses in Hollywood, all of whom were jostling for the best roles. Notoriety was part of her persona now.

Apart from continuing to carve out careers for themselves as actors, Bruce and Demi were also intent on making their mark on the other side of the camera – as producers. As is the wont of a significant proportion of Hollywood talent, the desire to be the master of one's own destiny is a goal that goes well beyond the realm of personal satisfaction. Warren Beatty, for example, was said to have made $30 million as producer and star of just three pictures, *Bonnie and Clyde*, *Shampoo* and *Heaven Can Wait*. After that, every actor who made it big eyed the supposedly greener grass on the other side with ambitious envy. Many were indulged by the major studios and were provided with their own production offices to explore scripts and proposals for possible future projects.

A few, like Michael Douglas, secured major deals. Douglas, that year, had just 'got into bed', as he termed it, with Columbia. His production company, Stonebridge, was contracted to produce two pictures a year for the next five years. Robert DeNiro, of course, had set up TriBeca in 1990 and soon had half a dozen movies in production. Robert Redford had long before created the Sundance Institute in Utah from which he was lately producing his own movies, like *The Milagro Beanfield War*. Clint Eastwood was doing much the same, skipping from one side of the camera to the other as producer, director and star in movies such as *Heartbreak Ridge, Bird* and *The Unforgiven*. And it wasn't just the men: Goldie Hawn, Bette Midler, Sally Field and Barbra Streisand had all produced their own projects.

When it was first rumoured the Willises were thinking about turning in that direction, however, the news was greeted by sections of the Hollywood establishment as being merely another sign of the couple's arrogance – why should they, mere newcomers, imagine it was either feasible or desirable to get involved behind the camera at such an early stage in their careers?

Critical voices wondered loudly what on earth Willis and Moore could have to contribute, apart from their wealth and notoriety. As one observer noted at the time, 'Bruce had been talking about making his own movie for years. He bought up a couple of projects, scripts and books, that never came to anything. He also had his script, such as it was, for the movie *Hudson Hawk*, that he had dreamed up years ago in New York. It was basically no more than a scribbled outline, pretty amateurish, but he was determined to try to get it made. Joel Silver, a producer with money and a keen eye for fresh talent, a sort of modern day Roger Corman, encouraged him and gave him a scriptwriter and the whole thing just moved on from there. Hudson Hawk Films suddenly became a reality and Bruce was jumping at the prospect of getting his movie made, with him involved in both production and as its star.'

Anxious not be left behind, Demi also turned her interest and determination to producing. She formed her own company, Rufglen Films, and linked up with an independent company in New York who had been touting around a screenplay called *Mortal Thoughts* for the last two years. In fact, it was on the set of *Ghost* that Taylor Hackford, the director of Richard Gere's *An Officer and a Gentleman*, handed Demi a copy of the script. He told her that he was looking for someone with whom to share production duties and asked if she was interested. She was, and promptly took the script home for Bruce to read.

'Every once in a while we ask one another to read scripts that we are considering,' Demi explained. 'At the time, Taylor had asked my agent about whether Bruce might be able to appear in the film, and when my agent asked me about it, I told him that he may as well forget it. Next thing I know, Bruce is coming to me and saying, "I want to play this guy."'

Bruce wanted to play the part of the evil James because, as Willis himself pointed out, 'He was such a bad guy. I had been playing all these heroes with a moral code and high standards. Well, I wanted to play a guy with no moral code and who had no sense of right and wrong. He was out on the edge and out of control.'

According to Demi, the protagonists in the feminist-orientated story were not, as far as Hollywood was concerned, in possession of the perceived vital attributes for box-office success. 'The writers were told that the script would get sold faster and would get made easier if it was about two men rather than two women,' she told *Empire* magazine. Two women, she sighed, 'were not going to cut it at the box office – or that's what the powers-that-be were saying,' during the script's two years in development hell.

But Demi stuck to her guns. 'There have always been good roles for women, but there are a lot more actresses than there are roles. It seems that there is a change taking place. In the recent past, we have seen films with women in the lead making some serious money,' she said. It certainly looked as though films with strong leading female characters were now back in vogue. Some half a dozen other movies with a woman as the main character were either in or approaching production, and it was the period that saw huge success for Jodie Foster's *Silence of the Lambs* and Geena Davis and Susan Sarandon in *Thelma and Louise*, among others.

With each partner now with a work-in-progress, Bruce and Demi were once again the talk of the Hollywood scene. There were any number of other actors and actresses, more established and respected than the Willises, who had spent years developing projects that, in the end, came to nothing. Demi and her husband, however, did not have that problem, and both found willing backers without very much effort on their part. Envious rivals wondered just how they had managed it.

Demi's movie, *Mortal Thoughts*, which beat Bruce's into production, was backed by Columbia Tristar, and her company was one of three independents involved. She would be the film's star, along with Glenne Headly who was fresh from working on *Dirty Rotten Scoundrels* and *Dick Tracy*. Willis took third billing and there was a strong support team that included Harvey Keitel, the

Willises' neighbour and close friend, in the role of Detective John Woods. He is the kind of actor, noted Taylor Hackford, 'who completely submerges himself in his role. He spent a great deal of time with homicide investigators and came to the set something of an expert. He is the surrogate for the audience. He's discovering the story right along with us.'

Demi had some trouble deciding which of the two leading female roles she would take. 'I went back and forth on that one,' she said. 'The role of Joyce seemed more intense. It was flashier. But ultimately I went with Cynthia because I perceived the challenge to be greater there. The complexities of the character were much more subtle. I also loved the idea of doing a New Jersey dialect because I had never done the Streep thing – an accent. I just saw Cynthia as the most specific and fleshed-out character I had ever played. Not like in *Ghost*, where I was the personification of emotion.'

As co-producer, Demi had nailed down a tough contract that gave her approval of both the cast and the script, and the right to hire and fire as she saw fit. She negotiated pre-production finance through bankers and then dealt personally with the studio moneymen and marketing and promotion experts. She even drew up the filming schedule, which was, in part, to accommodate the commitments of Bruce. 'I started cautiously,' she admitted, 'tiptoeing and learning as I went along, but suddenly I was in deep and involved in decisions that went right down the line. It was a good experience. But Bette Davis was right: when a man gives his opinion, he's a man; when a woman gives hers, she's a bitch.'

Certainly that was the consensus of opinion that emerged during the first week of filming, when co-writer of the screenplay and first-time director Claude Kerven quit the production over what Demi termed 'creative differences'. Alan Rudolph, best known at the time for *The Moderns* and *Love at Large*, was recruited to take his place. His arrival on the set improved things considerably, even though he had little time to prepare: 'I simply had no time to think, to plan, to mould. *Mortal Thoughts* became a creature of instinct for me. I had to leave the logistics to Demi. She was the one who got things done. And I still have this image in my mind of her, covered with blood from having just filmed the murder scene, negotiating with the production company for more money and time,' he recalled with a smile. 'She's the only producer I have ever known who really bled for her movie.'

And he had no doubts about her ability: 'She has an opinion on everything and she lets you know it. She's very, very smart, like a beautiful ballerina who can also kick box. But there's an honesty about her. She's absolutely straight, she and Bruce both. They come from some place that has a real truth about it. You go to their house and the warmth between them is totally genuine. I reckon that's their ultimate protection.'

Set in Bayonne, New Jersey, *Mortal Thoughts* was a suspense thriller about two friends, Joyce Urbanski (Headly) and Cynthia Kellogg (Demi), who have their hands full running Joyce's beauty salon while raising children and coping with their husbands. Cynthia clearly has an easier time of it than Joyce, who is tied to a husband (Willis) so abusive, aggressive and loud that almost everyone he meets wishes he would drop dead. So when he is murdered and his body found dumped in a ditch, family and friends feel everything from relief to sorrow to guilt. Naturally, the police centre their investigation on those who knew him best – his wife, Joyce, and her best friend, Cynthia. As the murder investigation closes in, conducted by Keitel's police detective John Woods, the strain begins to take its toll on the women's relationship, and friendship and morality begin to clash with the instinct for survival.

This was the theme that had intrigued co-screenwriter William Reilly. Having already examined the fine line between love and hate, need and revulsion in abusive relationships, he would now discover from sketching out the first draft another fascinating aspect of human behaviour. 'I found it very interesting how the police are able to interpret behaviour of the given individual by analysing the things a suspect says,' he explained. 'Certainly, this is how we came to use the process of interrogation in the film, to propel the story, and to use the police officers' sixth sense in deciphering what an individual's motives and objectives are.'

Demi was also thoroughly gripped by that issue, and her enthusiasm for the whole project spilled into her performance. It was in this movie more than any other, noted *Sight and Sound*, 'that we begin to see Moore open up a potential just glimpsed in her other work: that she can be a subtle and surprising actress as well as a compelling star. But, sadly, intelligent parts in little-seen Alan Rudolph films do not cement a star's position as an on-going Hollywood powerbroker.' That was true, as was the fact, disappointingly, that *Mortal Thoughts* was by no means a box-office smash, its gross of a little over $19,000,000 ranking it in a fairly low position on the year's most successful movies list.

The tabloid press, of course, were not particularly interested in whether the actress's performace was skilful or not. Although most did grudgingly credit her as the boss of her own movie, they were quick to suggest that the power had gone to her head and that her prima donna tendencies were now out of control.

Rumours would soon haunt Hollywood about how she wanted private planes, a suitable entourage of aides from secretaries to bodyguards, and limos at every point of her journeys to and from the West Coast.

When she heard that Douglas Thompson, a British writer resident in Los Angeles, had asked: 'Where does assertiveness begin and megalomania end, and where's the fine line between Sunset Boulevard and peel-me-a-grape indulgence?' her response was resistance. Finally, losing patience, Demi snapped, 'Yes, I want all those youthful, hopeful ambitions of childhood. Who doesn't? A lot of people want things but not everyone is willing to go out and get them. I am. It's hard walking away from opportunities now, chances I've been waiting for all my life. There are too many good actresses around to fill the roles for women. So you have to go out there and fight, pay attention, know what's going on. The reality is that you have to generate roles for yourself. That's right, and nobody will stop me now.'

For months afterwards, she became sick of always having to defend herself. Headlines of her autocratic stance, her petulant ways, and her 'GIMME MOORE' attitude were soon sharing top billing with her husband as the tabloids' number-one concern. She hated the salacious rubbish most of them published, well aware of just how pernicious their influence could be. In December 1990, when Bruce was filming *The Bonfire of the Vanities* in Rome, the Hollywood gossip mill announced he had become romantically involved with his co-star, Marushka Detmers, on the set of the movie. It was alleged that Willis incurred the wrath of his wife who demanded Detmers be fired immediately, or else. The truth was, of course, far less dramatic. According to her agents, the X-rated *Devil in the Flesh* actress had dropped out because she was suffering bouts of fainting fits and back problems. Publicly, Demi had nothing to say on the matter.

She was less reticent on the subject of her next two movie projects. By now, she had moved directly into shooting the first one, for Warner Brothers. Having proved with *Ghost* and *Mortal Thoughts* that she could hold her own in any company, it seemed only natural that, having played in the big leagues, Demi would continue there. Many people were surprised, therefore, when they heard she was taking fourth billing in Dan Aykroyd's latest picture, *Nothing But Trouble*, said to be a hilarious comedy.

Demi was not happy with the completed movie's eventual fate. If anything, it provided exactly what the title forecast. In its opening weekend, dominated by the débuts of other bigger movies, the film fell horribly flat. Heralded by reviews that were lukewarm at best, *Nothing But Trouble* earned just over $8 million in comparison to most of the others on release that same weekend, which raked in twice as much playing on fewer screens. As *Empire* magazine remarked so succinctly: 'In Dan Aykroyd's totally unfunny directorial début, hapless Demi is the dish Chevy Chase picks up and whisks off for a dirty weekend that never happens as they get nabbed by murderous weirdos led by Aykroyd and John Candy in drag. As career moves go, this can only be described as unfortunate for all concerned.'

The *Washington Post*'s Hal Hinson was of much the same opinion: 'It's nothing but trouble and agony and pain and suffering and obnoxious, toxically unfunny bad taste. It's nothing but miserable.'

A lot more promising – in pre-production at any rate – was *The Butcher's Wife*, the second of the two movies Demi had committed herself to shooting. Directed by Terry Hughes, another first-timer, Demi would play a clairvoyant who marries a New York butcher (played by George Dzundza) and then falls in love with a local psychiatrist, Alex (Jeff Daniels). Along the way, she warns her husband's customers about her premonitions concerning their lives. Even though one reviewer suggested that Paramount would have been better off if they had abandoned it altogether, British critic James Cameron-Wilson called the film 'a delightful, magical romantic comedy' but thought Demi 'was miscast as a naïve clairvoyant'.

(Interestingly enough, the film had originally been developed with Meg Ryan in mind as the lead role. But she had dropped out at the last minute when Demi was reported to be in negotiations for what turned out to be very favourable terms.)

Although the press and public would have agreed that she was in dire need of another hit, Demi's achievements so far seemed to have gone to her head. The rumour around the set was that she behaved like the star she thought she was, regardless of the fact that she had not yet really become one. The producers, it was said, pandered to her every whim. Aware that her success in *Ghost* could help carry their own movie, they went along with everything she asked for – everything from a dialogue coach, a masseuse in daily attendance and a psychic consultant who would be her guide in her clairvoyance, on top of the usual entourage of personal aides, make-up artist, hairdresser and stand-in.

She was also given a personal limo to take her to the studio and back, and even had a private plane to deliver her to and from locations. 'She's a very focused woman,' acknowledged the film's screenwriter Ezra Litwak. 'She is also very much a movie star and everything revolves around that fact. As far as the movie was concerned, she had a strong conception of the role and it wasn't up for discussion, period.'

But that wasn't the only problem Terry Hughes had to contend with as shooting got under way. On the first day of filming, for instance, Demi arrived on set with her hair blonde and announced that that was how she would be appearing in the movie. Whatever else, she didn't want audiences to be reminded of the delicate, doe-eyed character she had played in *Ghost*. But that proved to be the least of the director's difficulties. Having already seen the producers succumb to her every whim, he knew he would have a battle on his hands should he wish to make any script or directorial changes. As one set observer noted, 'He knew if he upset her, he might be sacked. He did get very angry, though, when she started handing out notes to other actors with hints on how they should play a particular scene.'

But when Hughes spoke out in print after filming was completed, accusing Moore of not being able to take direction and refusing his suggestions, Demi responded with disbelief. 'Very offensive. I was fighting to make a good movie, not crying for an orange juice on set.' The hints of bitterness did not auger well. With the movie due into the cinemas in the summer, soon after Willis's *Hudson Hawk* première, things couldn't have been worse.

# A SET OF STEAK KNIVES

*'I'm sure there are people who think I'm a bitch, but all I do is strive for perfection. I expect others to work as hard as me, but I'm not demanding to an unreasonable point'*
DEMI MOORE

Demi returned home to Idaho just before *The Butcher's Wife* was released, incredibly relieved that she had left Los Angeles. Away from the West Coast, she would be at least partially insulated from the expected fallout. The critics weren't too keen on the film and neither was the studio. In fact, test audiences and mass-market reviewers responded so poorly that it was agreed that the movie's best hope was for a fast and wide release. The studio heads didn't argue. If they released it ahead of the anticipated bad reviews, a quick opening weekend payoff might at least take some of the sting out of its failure – but so would a rush of publicity.

Demi herself had come up with the solution before the studio did. She knew she couldn't go on the talk circuit to promote *The Butcher's Wife* because she was now heavily pregnant with her second child, due around the film's release date – and anyway, she thought, the movie was probably beyond being talked up. What transpired would prove to be much more effective than any round of talk-show appearances could be, and went far beyond the studio's expectations. With a clinical analysis of her current situation, she decided the promotional effort should be focused on herself. The movie would be nothing more than the hook on which to hang it.

Demi already knew that *The Butcher's Wife* would do little to cement the star status temporarily granted to her by *Ghost*. It was a small movie with narrow appeal and totally uncontroversial. By now, she was nine years into her career, and should have followed *Ghost* with something that at least guaranteed to fill the box-office coffers. Instead, she had slammed herself into reverse. And, with her pregnancy keeping her off the screen for at least another year, she knew only too well that, unlike most leading men, women in Hollywood can fade into oblivion in shorter periods. She needed a sensation. As she had already proved as boss of her own production company, she knew she could achieve one. She did.

It probably helped that Demi was always thinking up ways to further her ambitions. One of her ideas was to get herself on the cover of one or two of the major glossies – not movie magazines as she had already done, but on some of the more general-readership ones such as *Life* and *Vanity Fair*. She had managed it before, when just sixteen years old, she had posed for a revealing spread of pictures in *Oui*, so why not now? After all, the 'Cindy Crawford Story' had at that time just featured in *Playboy*, with

Richard Gere's close friend and renowned celebrity photographer Herb Ritts virtually launching her into the heavens with a terrific set of topless photographs. It was what elevated Crawford out of simple modelling assignments and helped establish her as the genuine supermodel she was destined to become.

Months before her second child was due, Demi had agreed to be interviewed and photographed by *Vanity Fair*. At that time, Demi recalls, 'they asked me to do the cover after *The Butcher's Wife*. But I was blonde – we shot it and they weren't happy with it. When I came back I was pregnant.'

Later, out of a conversation with *Vanity Fair* photographer Annie Leibovitz came the idea for a set of photographs of her heavily pregnant to accompany the article, which was scheduled to be published around the time *The Butcher's Wife* hit the screens. It would be nothing seedy, of course, but glamorous and stylish instead. During the planning of the shoot with Leibovitz, Demi had thought of dressing in something sexy. 'Wouldn't it be kind of quirky to put a pregnant woman in black lingerie?' she had mused. They agreed it would be ideal for one of the photographs if she was to wear just a black lace bra and matching knickers. They did that as well.

They also decided to shoot something in her 'more natural state' – not semi-nude, but completely naked from head to foot. It seemed in keeping with her condition at that time. 'I did feel glamorous and beautiful and more free about my body,' she later told the *Vanity Fair* journalists. 'Bruce had a lot to do with that. He told me often that I was beautiful in pregnancy – and of course I wouldn't have done it at all if I'd felt it was morally questionable.'

Willis gave apprehensive approval and even agreed to a rare

interview about his wife for the article. The magazine's editors snatched the whole idea up. A posse of writers, photographers, make-up artists, hairdressers, haute-couturiers and jewellers descended upon the Willis household at Malibu and stayed for eight days. They dolled Demi up in high fashion and beachwear, adorned her in jewels lent by Laykin et Cie and gowns supplied by Neiman Marcus of Beverly Hills and photographed the actress in various poses, at the house and elsewhere.

In the end, the shot of Demi eight months pregnant, looking a model of glowing motherhood and wearing nothing but diamonds and a beautiful smile was published on the front cover of *Vanity Fair*'s August 1991 issue, and did indeed cause a sensation. No woman, the press told us, had ever been photographed naked and pregnant for anything other than a medical journal. Here for the first time in print media history was a celebrity in an iconic style that combined Hollywood imagery with that certain chic look which pregnancy was regarded at the time.

As a public-relations stunt it was classic. But it was also, lest we need reminding, a fake – fake, that is, when you consider that few women have the means to put such a gloss on their pregnant state by surrounding themselves with a small army of assistants, dressers and make-up artists. Demi tried to build-up the 'natural' way of pregnancy; she was very comfortable with it and nakedness was part of basic motherhood. Nature, in this case, had little to do with it, though, and what really showed through was not naked motherhood but naked ambition.

Although the editors of *Vanity Fair* were expecting a big reaction, even they were surprised at the outcome – as was Demi herself. Exceeding even Marilyn Monroe's *Playboy* calendar or

Natassja Kinski with nothing but a snake, the cover brought a worldwide reaction and Leibovitz's photograph was reproduced by virtually every major newspaper around the globe. There were many protests, too, from groups complaining about what they saw as the exploitation of 'this most precious gift', and in some Bible Belt towns across America news-stands were ordered to put a brown paper wrapper across the cover to hide Moore's naked and bulbous belly.

According to Demi, 'When Annie took the picture of me nude and pregnant, it was not for the magazine. It wasn't premeditated. We took it at the end of the session for me, for my family.' Besides, she continued, 'Annie had photographed me nude the first time I was pregnant. So when they asked me to do the *Vanity Fair* session, I thought about how people in this country don't want to embrace motherhood and sensuality. They're afraid to imagine a pregnant woman as sexy. So a lot of the responses to me being naked – although you saw nothing but a belly and a little bit of my butt – was realising that a sexy picture featured a belly that had a child in it. It's funny how when a child is born, it's this glorious moment in everyone's life, and you're the most wonderful woman that ever existed. But while you're pregnant, you're made to feel neither beautiful nor sexually viable. Women can either be sexy, or they can be a mother. I didn't want to have to choose, so I challenged that. I'm not the only one. There have been many women who've walked before me. So, believe me, I never set out to make any big statement.' But she did. As she herself would later point out, 'I love the irony of playing off the contrast of what I think is this fallacy – that because you're a mother, you're no longer sexy. And I certainly don't feel that way.' Was that why she agreed to it? Or was it just part and parcel of what Germaine Greer described as a woman who 'got to know her clitoris,' and according to another journalist, was now 'guaranteed to strike fear into the heart of many a modern man'?

Either way it was undeniable that as a public-relations exercise it had stunning results. In the USA alone, it was mentioned on 95 television stories, 64 radio shows, 1,500 newspaper articles and a dozen cartoons. Who used whom? Demi was quite frank about the commercial intent. 'I think we used each other,' she said. 'I would say, in the usage of each other, we were equal.'

And as for the article, 'I don't think I'm a big-time movie-star', she admitted to the journalist working for *Vanity Fair*. 'My career's been very slow. I've certainly not jumped into the superstar crowd, the flavour of the month. I don't know that it will ever happen . . . I want to have enough going on in my life – the real stuff – so I can roll with the ups and downs.'

With that knowledge, there came more self-awareness. She said she had come to the realisation that many people viewed her as a bitch. Was that because she asked for what she wanted? No, it wasn't. It was, she responded with characteristic fire, because 'I'm strong and opinionated, but not difficult in the sense that "My motor home [on set] isn't big enough." That kind of thing doesn't bother me. Besides, if you're a woman and you ask for what you want, you're treated differently than a man would be . . . it's a lot more interesting [for journalists] to write about me being a bitch than being a nice woman.'

While all this was going on Demi was distancing herself from her husband's recent troubles with his latest movie. It was essential that after the *Vanity Fair* pictures she should re-emerge as loudly as she could. 'The reviews of *Hudson Hawk* have been in-credibly malicious,' she snarled. 'But in truth it hasn't absorbed into anything going on for me. Obviously I have compassion for my partner and would prefer the response to be more positive. Other than that, I'm not involved with it.'

The first reviews of *The Butcher's Wife* that rolled in following its August 1991 release were much as the studio bosses expected. The film arrived in cinemas a week after Willis's *Hudson Hawk*, and disappeared just as quickly as his did. But even though it flopped, Demi had, of course, just experienced her sudden rise to international notoriety as the Nude Madonna Expecting Child. (The child, a daughter, was born during the same month as the film's release and was named Scout – not after Willis's flick *The Last Boy Scout* of that same year, but after a character from the classic American novel *To Kill a Mockingbird* by Harper Lee.) One of the immediate effects of this rise in her profile was that Demi was now on the short-list of actresses who read for director Rob Reiner's upcoming movie, *A Few Good Men*.

Based on a play that had been very successful on Broadway, it was the critically acclaimed story of a Navy lawyer's unrelenting quest to uncover the truth behind a military trial. The story begins when two young marines stand accused of murdering a member of their platoon during an unsanctioned disciplinary action known as a 'Code Red'. The Navy, in an effort to obtain a quick and quiet plea bargain, appoints Lieutenant J.G. Daniel Kaffee, a young, second-generation Navy lawyer, to defend the marines. Just fifteen months out of Harvard Law School, Kaffee has earned a reputation for glibness and a facility in plea-bargaining. Though possessed of a brilliant legal mind, he is more interested in softball games than in the hardball game of law.

At first the case appears routine: on the US Naval base at

Guantanamo Bay in Cuba – under the iron command of Colonel Nathan Jessep – two marines conduct a seemingly unauthorised punishment of a fellow soldier who has broken the chain of command by writing a letter to an off-base authority, threatening to report one of them for an illegal shooting over the fenceline.

Kaffee's defence team includes Lieutenant Commander Joanne Galloway who immediately questions her colleague's sense of commitment. Propelled by the courageous spirit that Kaffee lacks, Galloway refuses to allow him to choose the easy way out, pushing him deeper and deeper into the intricacies of the case. He soon realises that he must take the case to court, defying official expectations that he avoid an embarrassing trial. In the process, he grapples with his own personal lack of conviction, stemming from a life spent in the shadow of a highly respected and successful father, which has kept him emotionally distant and devoid of purpose. Kaffee becomes determined to unravel the mystery and bring to justice those responsible for the young marine's death, risking his professional career and challenging his own deepest fears.

Reiner would work with the same sense of determination in mind as he set about selecting his cast. Tom Cruise was the first actor on board, as Kaffee, and Jack Nicholson was recruited soon after as Colonel Jessep. The role of Joanne Galloway, however, was not so easy to fill. She had to be an actress who could be convincing enough as Kaffee's superior officer but without necessarily suggesting a romantic angle. According to casting director Jane Jenkins, Reiner felt any emotional bond between Kaffee and Galloway was better left implicit. 'We talked about Michelle Pfeiffer but decided that if you put two of the most beautiful people in the world together, the audience would be disappointed if there wasn't a love story.' Even though several actresses read for the part (including Julie Warner, Penelope Ann Miller, Elizabeth Perkins, Nancy Travis and Linda Hamilton), with Demi, Jenkins continues, there was 'a directness, a don't-even-flirt-with-me attitude that obliterated our concerns'.

Demi had, in fact, read for the part when she was about eight months pregnant. 'A month or two later, Rob called me and told me I'd got it. For me, a big part of this role was not playing into the stereotype of this kind of woman, which is one-dimensional. It was about finding her humanity. A lot of it was becoming comfortable with the words, so they became second nature, so it didn't seem that we were working hard. It was a mouthful at times. We did a lot of homework – the actors would get together before we started shooting and just run the words.'

That mouthful of words, she would most probably agree, occurred during the shooting of the movie's early stages, and was one of her finest moments in the film, when she questions Kaffee about his dedication to the case. What she wants to know is why, when his accused clients Dawson and Downey have been locked up since early morning, he's outside hitting a ball, and would he be very insulted if she recommended that different counsel be assigned. Why? Because she doesn't think he's fit to handle the defence.

But Kaffee, and more importantly Kaffee's supervisor, know otherwise. He has, after all, successfully plea-bargained forty-four cases in nine months. Besides, he tells her, 'You don't even know me.'

'You're wrong, I do know you,' she starts. 'Daniel Alistar Kaffee, born June eighth 1964 at Boston Mercy Hospital. Your father's Lionel Kaffee, former Judge Navy Advocate and

Attorney General of the United States, died 1985. You went to Harvard Law, then you joined the Navy, probably because that's what your father wanted you to do, and now you're just treading water for the three years you've got to serve, just kind of lying low until you can get out and get a real job. And if that's the situation that's fine, I won't tell anyone, but it's my feeling that if this case is handled in the same fast-food, slick-ass bizarre manner with which you seem to handle everything else, something's going to get missed, and I wouldn't be doing my job if I allowed Dawson and Downey to spend any more time in prison than absolutely necessary, just because their attorney had predetermined the path of least resistance.'

Apart from anything else, *A Few Good Men* would be the closest Demi had come so far in her career to a predetermined Hollywood mainstream movie, given that *Ghost* was an almost accidental runaway success. Although the salary didn't matter that much, it was still good enough to warrant her excitement – but then again, $3 million plus a slice of the action would be considered good by any stretch of the imagination.

Just two months after the birth of her second child, Demi now had a mere eight weeks to get back into shape before principal photography was due to begin on a chilly autumn day in Washington DC on 21 October 1991. She hired fitness guru Rob Parr, who had been Madonna's trainer on the singer's 'Blonde Ambition' world tour. He first started to work with Demi during the last stages of her pregnancy by gently putting her through a programme of swimming-pool exercises. But immediately after Scout's birth was when he really got down to business. First he started her on a schedule of sheer sweat and toil for three hours a day, seven days a week. And if that wasn't enough, every day for two months, Demi would push herself through a gruelling early-morning routine that began at 4 a.m. and included everything from running to biking, hiking, weight-training and swimming. It was, noted one observer, the whole body-honing thing.

By the time the production moved into the historic Culver City Studios, it was a different story. With Willis not far away on another set shooting the final stages of his own latest film, *Death Becomes Her*, with Meryl Streep and Goldie Hawn, the couple would often meet up in between takes, and at other times slip away on after-hour jaunts. And when they weren't doing that, they would fill their time by taking the kids to see the wild tigers on the set of Billy Crystal's new movie in production, *Mr Saturday Night*. In fact, the entire studio lot seemed to be crawling with children. The producers of *A Few Good Men* had set up crèche facilities to accommodate the offspring of those attached to the movie. Apart from Demi's two, there was also Jack Nicholson's two children by Rebecca Broussard, Rob Reiner's baby son, and co-star Kevin Bacon's son, who also got to be in the movie.

Other aspects of life on the set might not have been quite so harmonious, though. Tom Cruise, the headlining player, had a clause written into his contract that stipulated he would have the trailer nearest to the set. Believe it or not, such details matter in Hollywood. Nicholson was next, and third in line was Demi. But she asked the studio to reconsider. First of all, she asked for and eventually got a double-sized trailer because she wanted to have her children with her at all times, plus the children's nannies, plus Daneen Conroy, her friend and employee for the past six years. Daneen was Demi's personal assistant, bodyguard, telephone answering service, rebutter of unwanted approaches from

TOP LEFT: As a child Demi considered herself a skinny, spectacled 'cross-eyed clumsy ugly duckling.'

TOP RIGHT: With clothes pretty much typical of other kids, 'I was always a little bit kind of nerdy,' said Demi of her childhood

RIGHT: Although Demi was very self-conscious about her right eye, which crossed over slightly, it didn't stop her pursing a career in modelling and acting.

Demi was only 13 when she discovered the truth that her real father had been married and dumped by her mother all in the space of two months.

Although Demi made her modelling début at 16, it didn't provide her with the big break she had hoped for. She remained as anonymous as the thousands of other girls trying for the same lucky break.

After dropping out of high school and the period modelling in Europe, Demi was drawn, through necessity, to Hollywood to try out for bit-parts in film and television.

Demi's provocative shots, wearing practically nothing for the titillating men's magazine *Oui*, were a far cry from the foxtress poses she would later take on in her bid for greater exposure.

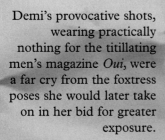

Demi's first television appearance of note was as a regular in the top-rated daytime soap *General Hospital*, in which she played Jackie Templeton – a role that would eventually launch her on the road to stardom as an actress.

LEFT: In February 1980 Demi (pictured here in her wedding dress) married rock musician Freddy Moore, who later spoke bitterly about their time together.

BELOW: Demi fell in love with co-star Emilio Estevez on the set of *St Elmo's Fire* (1985), but although they set a pre-Christmas wedding for the following year, Demi called the whole thing off just weeks after the invitations had gone out.

TOP: Demi and Bruce's first child together, a daughter they named Rumer after authoress Rumer Godden, was born on 16 August, 1988.

ABOVE: Although Demi would have little contact with her mother, Virginia Guynes, they are shown here together (with baby daughter Rumer) in 1988. 'I don't have any contact with her,' Demi later said. 'I don't really relate to my mother at all.'

Demi was eight months pregnant with her second child,
Scout, when she appeared nude on the cover of *Vanity Fair*'s
August 1991 issue.

With a critical thumbs-up and a box-office two-fingers in the US, *Mortal Thoughts* (1991) was released in Britain to much the same reaction: it marked Demi's twelfth movie in ten years, her début as a producer and her first with husband Bruce Willis.

By 1992, Demi and Bruce Willis had become the focus of renewed attention as the most talked about, most written about, most admired, and most hated couple in Hollywood.

press, photographers and fans, and general gofer on call twenty-four hours a day. She even had an assistant of her own to help out. Demi also wanted her trailer to be closest to the set, so that she could dash back and forth to see her children at any time during the long days of filming. Nicholson conceded he didn't give a damn where he was located and, in the end, neither did Cruise, so Demi moved to the front of the line. But when *Empire* magazine caught up with her for an interview in May 1993, it seemed none of this was true. 'Never once was my trailer closer than Tom's and never once did I ask for it to be moved. There's a standard rule: first star is the closest, and Tom was first star.'

Happily, on this occasion, there was no tension either between actress and director. The only time Reiner would have stood firm on his role as director and co-producer was in his decision not to have love scenes of any kind between Kaffee and Galloway. As far as he was concerned, there would be no kissing, no bedroom wrestling and certainly no nudity or even semi-nudity. It would be just a straightforward drama that, at best, would only hint at a developing relationship between the two characters played by Cruise and Moore. Although Reiner openly admitted he was slightly apprehensive at first about casting Demi – based on the 'difficult' reputation that preceded her – he experienced no problems, much to his relief. 'She had all the qualities I was looking for, strength and sexuality, which was crucial. She was sharp and intelligent,' he said. Even Jack Nicholson, whose brilliance is often regarded as intimidating by his co-stars, liked her too.

Reiner, once an actor himself, considered Demi to be a far better actress than most of the movies she had made up to that point would suggest, and to this day continues to defend her against the back-biters. 'I know from personal experience what actors go through when they are as intelligent as the powers-that-be. What comes out is a person who is being difficult, when all they are trying to do is make a decent movie.'

Demi was equally enamoured with Reiner: 'I so respect him as a director that I really wanted to be good for him. I read the script, but I had questions about it. Then I read the play and realised some of the things I questioned had been taken out. But I wanted to be kind of delicate because I was getting this reputation for being too assertive. So when I auditioned for Rob, he was actually scared because he'd heard all these rumours about me. He actually called two or three directors I'd worked with, but I'm glad to say most, if not all, of his concerns were dispelled.'

Despite the general good feeling on set, the critical reaction on the movie's release was far from wholehearted. Sometimes, though, it doesn't matter what the critics think. Sometimes the cinema-going public is perfectly capable of making up its own mind. With a $158 million gross in the US alone, the sound of popcorn mingled with the gnashing of critical teeth as literally acres of unsympathetic newsprint were trampled in the aisles of America's cinemas. Rob Reiner's *A Few Good Men* enjoyed one of the biggest box-office runs in Columbia Pictures' history.

Writing in the *Chicago Sun-Times* in December 1992, critic Roger Ebert was not surprised that many reviewers were so unsympathetic to the film. It was 'one of those movies that tells you what it's going to do, does it, and then tells you what it did. It doesn't think the audience is very bright. There is one scene that is absolutely wrong. In it, a lawyer played by Tom Cruise previews his courtroom strategy to his friends. The strategy then works as planned – which means that an element of surprise is missing from the most important moment in the movie, and the key scene by Jack Nicholson is undermined, robbed of suspense and made inevitable.' And that's a shame, as the disappointed Ebert put it, 'because in many ways this is a good film, with the potential to be even better than that. The flaws are mostly at the screenplay level; the film doesn't make us work, doesn't allow us to figure out things for ourselves, is afraid we'll miss the clues if they're not spelled out.'

By the time Demi had presented herself for work on the set of *A Few Good Men* in that autumn of 1991, film producer Keith Barish, best known for his later work on Harrison Ford's *The Fugitive*, and Robert Earl, the world's most successful restaurateur, were going into partnership to launch Planet Hollywood. Their idea was to open a series of showbiz-themed eateries not too far removed from the musicbiz concept of the already established Hard Rock Café (with which, incidentally, Earl had previously been involved). The main difference was that Planet Hollywood would be aimed at 'capitalising on the universal appeal of movies, sports and other entertainment-based themes'.

Earl had the ingenious idea of offering share options to a handful of movie stars in exchange for their participation in promoting new openings and endorsing their products. Although Demi would not become one of the shareholders for another two years, Bruce Willis, Arnold Schwarzenegger, Sylvester Stallone and Whoopi Goldberg did. The deal was that they would take a slice of the equity and, in due course, the profits in exchange for lending their names to the company and carrying out certain duties, namely, according to its prospectus: 'to frequently attend grand openings of new Planet Hollywood units as well as other special events at the units, thereby generating significant media attention and publicity for the Planet Hollywood brand. Moreover, as a result of the popularity and high visibility of the Planet Hollywood units, the motion-picture community would frequently use the units as sites for well-publicised movie promotions and other celebrity-sponsored events.'

The first of these 'units' was opened in Washington DC that same October with all five stars attending, mixing with guests and signing autographs and T-shirts. It was the beginning of an international bonanza for the stars, not to mention the original founders of the company, as the chain proceeded to expand to major cities throughout the world and at which – evident from the resultant publicity – the Schwarzenegger-Stallone-Willis triumvirate would be especially active. No opportunity to promote the Planet Hollywood franchise would be overlooked. Well, not according to the prospectus, it wouldn't. It noted: 'The company has promoted its brands primarily through the operation of theme restaurants, which provide a unique dining and entertainment experience in a high-energy environment, and their integrated retail stores, offering a broad selection of premium-quality merchandise displaying the company's logos.'

Over the next five years, the company expected to have a total of 51 restaurant-merchandise stores up and running in 16 different countries. They would typically be located at high-profile sites in major tourist areas such as Walt Disney World in Orlando, Caesar's World Forum Shops in Las Vegas, Piccadilly Circus in London and the Champs-Elysées in Paris.

While the restaurants were the main attraction, the sales from its merchandising stores to this day produce the highest profits from selling jackets, T-shirts, sweatshirts and baseball caps. The future was in the stars, literally.

And 'stars' remains the word that best describes the opening of a Planet Hollywood franchise. It feels like it's Oscar night all over again. Usually the crowds outside will have been gathering since dawn, anxious for a place on the pavements as near as possible to their idols who are expected to turn up, and even the ones that aren't. The police will have been out since early morning, putting up barricades and cordoning off streets. With the millons of dollars' worth of movie talent scheduled to arrive, they take no risks. Even the sniffer dogs used by the bomb squad will have done their job around the place, and plain-clothed detectives will have scanned the faces of the fans for the one crazed lunatic who might want to claim his 15 minutes of fame.

When they opened the restaurant in Hollywood itself, on the corner of Wilshire Boulevard and Rodeo Drive, for example, the scenes were likened to a royal visit or a presidential address to the nation. To kick off proceedings, Arnie, Sly, Bruce and Demi turned up (an hour behind schedule) to attend a press conference at the Regent Beverly Wilshire Hotel, at which 300 journalists and photographers from around the world were waiting patiently. Accompanied by Planet Hollywood executives and a ring of bodyguards, they were, said some observers, like the high-powered leaders of a business conglomerate about to report on their company's annual performance.

The restaurant had the added glittering attraction of being where visitors could expect to find the largest collection anywhere in the world of authentic movie memorabilia. Sharon Stone's ice pick from *Basic Instinct*, Val Kilmer's *Batman Forever* suit, Marilyn Monroe's gown from *Gentleman Prefer Blondes* and Judy Garland's dress from *The Wizard of Oz* were all displayed among the celebrity palm-print walls, the 'coming soon' trailer previews and the music soundtracks pumped out in between. There were even some artefacts from the shareholders' movies.

The menu, or 'dining experience' as it was known, reflected their good taste – from the freshly prepared foods of the new Californian classic cuisine, to pastas, exotic salads, turkey burgers (one of Demi's favourites), pizzas, vegetarian dishes, blackened shrimp, fish, smoked and grilled meats. And if that wasn't enough there was a wide range of tempting desserts including the Schwarzenegger apple strudel (made from his mother's renowned recipe), and another Demi favourite, caramel crunch pie. It was the kind of place no one could resist, whether they were a shoeshine boy or a superstar.

# HOLLYWOOD
# SERENADE

*'I realised that women who lack self-esteem are lost. I
was determined never to relinquish my power again. My
sexuality and my sensuality are part of that power,
especially in Hollywood'*

DEMI MOORE

Taking it one step at a time, Demi and Bruce put their minds to
moving again. They began looking for a new home as far
removed from life on the East and West Coasts as they could
possibly find. By the early months of 1992 they had found what
they were searching for: a six-bedroom, seven-bathroom ranch
set on 48 acres of beautiful surroundings on the outskirts of
Hailey, a former gold-rush community that nestles in the valley
of the snow-capped Sawtooth Mountain. Situated a few miles
from Idaho, and 900 miles from Beverly Hills, the Willises were
thrilled.

Hailey was, and still is, a typical American town of its kind. It has one main street with shops serving a population of 3,687. The couple had first come across the place eight years earlier when they visited Sun Valley, the celebrity-favoured winter resort area. In fact, the valley had been attracting movie stars since the 1930s, but somehow the little town of Hailey, which started life in the 1880s around a clutch of gold and silver mines, was overlooked. It was like a town from the 1950s – unhurried and largely unaffected by the pressures of the outside world.

In no time at all, they had the ranch renovated, built a garage big enough to house their collection of vintage cars and motor-cycles and settled horses into the stables. The couple then turned their attentions to the town itself, where the main street was looking in much need of restoration. Demi and Bruce began purchasing a number of the properties there, several of which had been so completely neglected that they were in a severe state of deterioration and disrepair. The Willises were embarking upon a real-estate shopping spree which would continue over the next three years. They invested more than $13 million in property, and every time they purchased another piece of Hailey's Main Street they had it restored to its former glory and installed a new business in it.

Bruce had first been attracted to a bar named The Mint. It was an old miners' hangout on Main Street and still attracted the town's rougher elements. He had taken his band there one Saturday night for a gig, possibly with the same line up of musicians that he had used for his first Motown album, *The Return of Bruno* in 1986 (which, interestingly enough, had included the original members of the Temptations on harmonies) and probably the same ones who played with him on some other gigs, one before a crowd of 22,000. The only downside here was that the place erupted into a brawl. He later bought the freehold, closed the bar down, gutted the inside and set about turning it into a smart 160-seat bistro trimmed with Peruvian mahogany, and had the walls covered with vintage movie-stills and posters. Strangely for a bistro, there was also a pool room, a sauna and a steam room. Demi refurbished the upstairs into a quiet, relaxing lounge with deep sofas and soft décor. It was all very glamorous but, as local newspaper editor Dan Gorham noted, it seemed a pretty lavish place for their small town and there wasn't much hope of it making money. As far as the Willises were concerned, that didn't matter. And, as if to prove the point, not too long afterwards they were negotiating to buy four more properties on Main Street. One was the now broken-down Liberty Cinema for which they had grand ideas. Another was a parcel of land opposite, where Demi planned to build a museum to house her own collection of two thousand dolls. If that wasn't enough, there was also a large, decaying block which they would rename the E.G. Willis Building after Bruce's grandfather. It would be remodelled to include professional offices, craftsmen's studios and a 1950s-style Shorty's Diner. They also talked of building a sixty-five-room hotel.

According to Gorham, the town's residents pretty much left the pair alone to get on with it. They were seen as just ordinary folk with money, and the view of the townspeople overall was generally supportive of their property-buying spree – even if some did fear the Hollywood connection would attract an unwanted tourist element to the place. It no doubt helped matters when Willis told the locals that he and his wife were not expecting to make money from the redevelopment. If anything, their interest was in the town itself, and they hoped their investment would provide employment for the local community.

The couple were allowing themselves very little time for any Hollywood-style frivolities. But some gossip-columnists were hinting that maybe they were keeping a low profile because of a case made in the Small Claims court against Demi six months earlier by Deborah Hellman. Hellman, of Dolls Etcetera in Los Angeles, alleged that the actress had picked up a doll valued at $7,000 from her on approval. When she returned it, apparently, it was minus its wood base. Hellman had demanded the payment, which had not been forthcoming, and she consequently sued to recover the value of the base, which she claimed was worth $600. In the end, after one postponement, the court entered a judgement against Demi. She had nothing to say on the matter, offering neither a denial nor an explanation, not even in the following letter she wrote, on Ruflgen Films notepaper, to the Court Administrator.

Dear Mr Guillen:

I am writing to the Small Claims Court requesting that the Court postpone the hearing scheduled on this matter on December 15, 1992. I will be out of town at my residence in Idaho with my two young children on December 15, 1992 and will not be returning to Los Angeles any sooner than February 1, 1993. In fact, I was out of town at my residence in Idaho at the time that the Small Claims Summons was left at my office.

I will be substantially prejudiced if there is no postponement of this hearing from December 15, 1992 until a later date, since I will be unable to defend the claim to present my evidence to dispute the meritless claim. There is no money that is owed to the Plaintiff. I am respectfully requesting that you postpone the hearing to allow me the opportunity to defend this claim since no money is owed to the Plaintiff.

I would appreciate it if you would grant my request to postpone the hearing date to a date after February 1, 1993.

Thank you for your anticipated courtesy and co-operation in this matter.

Sincerely,
Demi Moore

By that summer of 1992, both Bruce and Demi were preparing to leave their rural retreat and go back to work. Willis, who had now been absent from the screen for at least a year, had finally concluded a new picture deal, which looked good on paper at least. It was a project for producer Arnon Milchan, with a working title of *Three Rivers*, later changed to *Striking Distance*. Filming would commence that autumn for release exactly one year later.

Demi, in comparison, would have two films released in the same period. *A Few Good Men* was due to hit the screens in December 1992, with *Indecent Proposal* due out in the following April. As far as she was concerned, Adrian Lyne's movie was the crucial one. It would bring her two things she had so longed for: a pay cheque of $5 million (her biggest to date) and, more importantly, entry into the Hollywood superstar league. With second billing to Robert Redford, how could she fail?

But, before that, she concluded that her public profile would benefit from another timely boost: to signal her forthcoming rise to eminence, and to let the world know, too, that Bruce Willis was alive and well and about to start working on a new movie. Once again she went into a huddle with photograper Annie Leibovitz who had produced her pregnancy pictures almost a year earlier. She seemed prepared to forgive *Vanity Fair* for the 'horrible' article that had accompanied that bodily exposure. (At the time she had objected to the writer raking over her past, and even more to some bitchy quotes from industry insiders.) All the same, they were now plotting another big hit together.

That old Hollywood adage about all publicity being good publicity held good for her. Indeed, Demi had already made a clinical study of the publicity machine that operated during the golden age of Hollywood, discovering how the studios and the stars always worked together to achieve maximum impact for whatever movie they were promoting at the time or to enhance the image of a star. She, too, had worked out her own technique for media manipulation, attempting to gain a measure of control over the presentation of herself to the public and of the photo-graphic approval in exchange for her co-operation. It didn't always work, as she couldn't always have the final say in the editorial matter of a magazine like *Vanity Fair*. She had no choice but to accept what they wrote. Some, however, like *Hello!*, were willing to be uncontroversial just to be guaranteed an interview.

She was now working on another news-stand special for the cover of *Vanity Fair*. And once again she was going naked, to demonstrate how she had transformed herself from nude Madonna to sleek siren. As ever, she wanted it done with style and sophistication – but with a completely different approach to the last cover. At the time, body painting was all the rage, and who better to consult for ideas than one of the most pre-eminent exponents of that art, Joanne Gair. She pondered for a while and then produced her masterplan: Demi's entire body would be painted to look as though she were wearing a man's suit.

And so, just ahead of the release of *A Few Good Men*, her publicity coup, the likes of which a thousand professional publicists in Hollywood could only dream of, was set in motion. Once again, a posse of aides descended upon her, courtesy of *Vanity Fair*. The body painting by Joanne Gair took a mammoth 15 hours to complete and then a further two hours to photograph. 'The time-consuming part,' said Gair, 'was building up the density of paint and maintaining the pattern of the cloth before it melted through the body heat. But Demi was really into it.'

With the photographs completed, the actress then co-operated for another article to accompany them, which would run over five pages of the August 1992 issue of the magazine. This time, she agreed to be observed and interviewed in her home, at work, over lunch and so on, for the verbal picture of her lifestyle. Willing to accept the intrusion of the interviews at the time, she was once again not so happy with the resultant article.

From her point of view, *Vanity Fair* had carried the usual sting in the tail to make the point that this wasn't a promo piece. The article even quoted studio executives who complained that Demi had caught her husband's worst habits of making demands. The writer recorded that during a two-hour interview at home, a parade of household staff had passed by, once again emphasising the existence of the couple's 'entourage'. It was no secret by then, anyway. Willis himself had said they had twenty-seven people working for them, including staff at their joint offices in Beverly

Hills and their home in Hailey. But, according to an unnamed friend who was quoted in the feature, 'They are never alone. If you ask me, it's a pretty weird marriage and a pretty weird way to live, surrounded by other people all the time.' But it was probably the last line of the piece that irritated Demi most: she wanted 'good work, things to be the best they can . . . I want greatness'.

Although afterwards she moaned bitterly about the tone of the article – saying, 'It took eight days of my life including another body shooting, which they didn't use. It's not that I need to have a sugarcoated story. It's just a matter of attitude' – she was also honest enough to acknowledge her motives for doing it in the first place. Now, she could see the value in what many regarded as another typical piece of Moore exhibitionism. 'When I walked away from it, I discovered the advantage to me was that people only remembered the photograph – not the words.'

What followed for Demi was not about greatness or even fine acting, though, and certainly not about an especially good film. She became the tangible focus of the hype that surrounded *Indecent Proposal* and its one basic concept that was suddenly intriguing married couples around the globe: 'What would you do if someone offered a million dollars to spend the night with your partner?' Spawned by the film-making combination of producer Sherry Lansing and director Adrian Lyne, it turned into an international controversy, just as their work together on *Fatal Attraction* had done five years earlier.

Demi's movie was the brainchild of Sherry Lansing, who at that point was one of the industry's most powerful producers. She first came to prominence in the industry as the first female president of a Hollywood studio, as head of production at 20th Century Fox in 1980. Across town was her partner, Stanley Jaffe, who had much the same position at Paramount. At just twenty-nine years of age, he ensured his reputation as the youngest studio head in Hollywood history. By 1987 they were producing their own features as independents, Michael Douglas's controversial *Fatal Attraction* and Jodie Foster's Oscar-winning *The Accused* among them. The latter was probably one of the most successful films to support the ever-growing cause of feminism and address the issues surrounding rape, even though it would be true to say both it and *Fatal Attraction* were accused of exploitation.

So, drawn to success and controversy, it was no surprise that Lansing should team up again with Lyne for *Indecent Proposal*, a movie with a plot that could be pitched in a single sentence without leaving anything out: struggling newly-weds go to Las Vegas with all the money they possess, try to double it, lose the lot, agree to a millionaire's offer of a million dollars for a night with the young wife, then split up in the anguished aftermath.

It was released during 'Hollywood's Year of the Woman', a celebration in which Lansing herself would play a prominent role. It was not, she and the director insisted, an exploitative film – she would be 'shocked and hurt' at the very suggestion – but one which explored the reactions of a woman faced with such a situation, and being torn between the very different responses of the two men.

It was dismissed in some circles as a cynical Hollywood packaging exercise manufactured by the deal-makers who delivered three names, a director and a script into a studio which, in the pre-production hype, had the added guaranteed attraction of Demi Moore direct from her nude appearance on the front cover of *Vanity Fair*. How on earth could they fail?

Lyne, of course, bridled at such suggestions. 'Horseshit!' he screamed. He said he was never dictated to that way. He went for Robert Redford because it was the kind of role that audiences would not expect from him. Woody Harrelson, best known at the time for his role as a naïve barman in television's *Cheers* sitcom, was recruited for what Lyne described as the essential innocence of the character: 'He was the kind of guy that audiences could forgive.'

MGM, however, could not forgive him. By the time Harrelson was negotiating for the part in Lyne's film, he had already signed to do Johnny Depp's *Benny and Joon*, and was at that point said to be in breach of his contract, and seriously delaying the production of a major motion picture. The studio intended to make him painfully aware of that. Harrelson was promptly sued for $5 million and threatened with an injunction if he were to play any other role during the period he should have been filming *Benny and Joon*. Harrelson countered with a claim he couldn't work with that film's director, Jeremiah Chechik. MGM were not convinced and their lawsuit contained what they believed to be the true circumstances behind his departure: 'Sudden success has caused Harrelson to attempt to take advantage of his new popularity by disregarding his existing obligation in favour of another motion picture project he now considers more favourable.' Eventually, though, Harrelson's gamble paid off; formerly television's affable bartender and very little else, suddenly he was a star of what became one of that year's most successful movies in America.

The main character, the wife at the centre of Redford's indecent proposal, was difficult to cast. Although the director had sat through several auditions with other actresses such as

Nicole Kidman, Annabella Sciorra and even British singer Lisa Stansfield, when he watched Demi reading for the part, he knew his search had ended there and then – even though at that point he had already decided on another actress. To complicate matters further, for Lyne at any rate, was the fact that he openly admitted that he had never really liked Demi – presumably he meant as an actress. She had read for every one of his past movies and had never been called back. This time, though, something clicked as she and a stand-in for Harrelson role-played the scene where they are in bed together discussing the million-dollar offer and whether or not they should accept it. Lyne was simply enthralled by her relaxed performance. He also liked the way she looked – 'kind of Rubenesque', he said – after having her baby.

Filming began at the end of August 1992 on the Paramount lot and later on location in Las Vegas. But Lyne, like others before him, was aware of the 'difficult' reputation that preceded his leading lady, and soon found the rumours had some substance. Once again, she had seen her character as being resilient, a bit like her role in *A Few Good Men*. But Lyne did not agree. If anything, he believed, she should be vulnerable. 'We pulled and pushed and tugged, which was perhaps not a bad thing,' he remembered. 'At the time, I thought, "God, is anything worth this pain?" Half the time . . . I could have murdered her.'

But when *Empire* magazine caught up with the actress after filming was completed, Demi responded, 'He and I had friction over my constant need to fight to make my character smarter, to show her more in control of the decisions that are made. I don't want to say that Adrian's chauvinistic, but he has a more traditional sense of women. We actually laugh about it now, but there was a scene where I wanted to keep my clothes on, and I told him, "They don't have to see my breasts in every shot, do they?" I don't know if he means to be offensive to women, I just think it's how, out of his passion, he romanticises them. We'd literally be talking, loudly sometimes, about the same thing. It's worked out, we have a tremendous affection for each other. I can only try as much as I can to portray this character as being as well grounded as I hope she'll be, but in the end I'm at the mercy of how Adrian cuts it together.' She needn't have worried.

She also had to deal with the movie's sexual content, particularly the session on the kitchen floor, in which the characters played by Demi and Harrelson make love. At one point, stripped and naked, she announces his pants are on fire. 'That's the worst stuff you have to do,' she recalled with a smile. 'Woody is one of Bruce's friends. I mean, he's been to my house and played with the kids. He said, "It's hard to think of you in an attractive way; you're my friend's wife." At the same time, there's a natural comfort built in because we know each other, just our physical rapport.'

Nonetheless, the world was grateful. Released in April 1993, *Indecent Proposal* was yet another of Demi's movies which predictably attracted criticism. 'So unintentionally silly, so thoroughly implausible, all you can do is bow your head in astonishment,' wrote the *Los Angeles Times*. 'Unredeemably awful,' agreed British film critic Philip French in his condemnation of the film. The *Washington Post* considered the film 'a monstrosity'. Desson Howe shuddered that 'director Lyne, whose *Fatal Attraction* looks celestial by comparison, indulges in such fraudulent morality you assume he's kidding'. Not every review was entirely negative, however. One described *Indecent Proposal* as 'ridiculously corny, often strangely compelling and never less than entertaining, it may lose its bottle towards the end but at least it had some bottle to start with'.

The press were swift to dub it another *Honeymoon in Vegas*, refering to the Andrew Bergman film released the previous year where Nicholas Cage played a goofball fearful of committing to marriage until he loses fiancée Sarah Jessica Parker to millionaire gambler James Caan in a poker game. Such comparisons were not really justified, though. As far as Demi was concerned, '*Honeymoon in Vegas* was a broad comedy; *Indecent Proposal* is a morality play.' Not only that, she continued, 'but in the first script the Redford character was an ugly, stereotypical user, the rich guy without morals, values or ethics. In the rewrite, he became a handsome, charming guy, to whom challenging someone else's morals is a game. Then he falls in love with someone he can't have. It's much more multi-layered.'

Adrian Lyne, understandably soured by the critics' scorn, bitterly complained that they had missed the film's point altogether. It was, he snapped, intended as pure escapism. The theme, rather than the quality of the movie, however, caught public imagination. As with *Fatal Attraction*, it inspired an international media debate with thousands of headlines and articles on the rights and wrongs of 'What would you do if . . . ?' Countless television chat-shows took up the idea, and Oprah Winfrey even managed to find enough people who'd had similar proposals in real life to devote an hour-long special to the subject. But, once again, it didn't matter what the critics thought. The cinema-going public gave it the thumbs-up, and with a combined box-office and video-rental gross of over $200 million worldwide, the film could hardly be considered a flop.

Nor did it go completely unappreciated in the plethora of award shows with which Hollywood now abounds. Not for the first time in her career, Demi (with Harrelson, of course) narrowly won the Best Kiss prize this time over Ethan Hawke and Winona Ryder's nomination for *Reality Bites* at the MTV's annual movie awards.

Demi, of course, lapped up the hype as she travelled around the globe to promote the movie. She was accompanied by an infantry of studio executives and public-relations staff, fronted by her own publicist, Pat Kingsley, whose role was not so much to ensure publicity as to guard against the unwanted kind. Demi was warned to expect a fiery reception, especially in London. She did indeed face a less-than-rapturous welcome from the 60 journalists who crowded into her press conference to bombard her with questions. But she fielded all of them with a quiet confidence, batting back the ones she didn't want to answer with ease.

'How do you feel about your husband's vilification by the media?' someone asked.

'That probably affects you more than me,' she replied.

Clearly anticipating a critical response, the actress and her advisers insisted on strict guidelines for any journalist requesting a one-to-one interview. First and foremost, they would have to sign an undertaking that they would not ask questions of a personal nature. Why, if she was so guarded, was she subjecting herself to this world tour of interrogation? In answer to that, she was as candid and honest as ever: she was doing it for herself, pushing towards her ultimate goal. If, by her efforts, more people came to see the movie, it would help her own career. She would then have a greater choice of roles, and could select the ones she wanted to do. It was all about control. Above everything else, the Demi Moore press junkets for *Indecent Proposal* were about *her*. She hadn't edged her way into the superstar stakes for nothing.

She was now firmly ranked among the top ten box-office stars of the decade – and just at the very moment, interestingly enough, that her husband faced the possibility of dropping out of the same rankings. In fact, it was down to Demi to provide a more positive insight into the movie family Willis that winter of 1993. By then pregnant with her third child, she appeared on *The David Letterman Show* and, amid hysterical whoops and cheers from the audience, she was announced as the 'most successful actress working today'. The basis for that assessment was not so much an artistic comparison with her peers as the fact that 'her last two movies have earned almost half a billion dollars'. The audience screamed with delight. Money, money, money. It's the American dream, and she was now its epitome. She sat there, small but drop-dead gorgeous, and talked about her work and her family. 'Bruce is fine, working hard as usual', she said, and discussed how they strove to spend quality time together with their children.

A month or so later, Demi took steps to ensure that she would not be forgotten during her impending temporary absence from the screen. She won herself another lavish spread in *Vanity Fair*. When she looked back at the previous sagas, she promised herself it was something she would never repeat. But, then again, over six pages of the December issue, under the headline 'DEMI'S STATE OF GRACE', she could at least reveal how she evolved her Rufglen Films into a new production company, Moving Pictures, naming her best friend Suzanne Todd as its president and Bruce's brother David as an executive. It would produce her next picture, *The Scarlet Letter*, to be made in 1994, after her third baby had been delivered. 'Having it all,' she repeated, smiling wistfully, 'just means having things that make you happy.'

One of those 'things', according to *Variety*, was her determination to break some of the traditional industry moulds. 'Movie-stars with production companies have become a regular fixture in Hollywood,' explained reporter Colin Brown. 'It is where the majors frequently pamper their most successful acting talent with well-furnished and fully staffed offices in the hope of developing a lucrative working relationship. Many are no more than vanity deals that bear little production fruit; others are derided by industry executives for churning out material that merely shows off their star presidents.'

Neither was true in Demi's case. 'One of Moving Pictures' goals is to develop material that I don't appear in,' she insisted. 'It is a much harder task to get someone to green-light a picture when you're a producer or have a production company than it is if you're going to be in it.'

She had already singled out projects that would have a high proportion of women both on screen and behind the camera, and be targeted at female audiences. 'In addressing the problem of the lack of roles for women, I have become very interested in trying to develop material for other women,' she reasoned. 'It's not that there aren't pictures where there are strong female characters and it's not that there aren't pictures that appeal to women. It's just that, on balance, there are not enough. We're just trying to adjust the deficit, as opposed to simply complaining that there's nothing out there.'

# RISKY
# ROLES

*'What we really go to the movies for is the heightened romance, the sensuality, the touching and stroking, more or less the foreplay'*

DEMI MOORE

By 1994 Demi almost had Hollywood at her feet. The success of *Indecent Proposal*, with its $200 million gross, and the upcoming *Disclosure* movie, her most recent project, had firmly established her among the upper echelon of Hollywood actresses. Although she hadn't yet carried a movie on her name alone, she nevertheless continued to strike a profitable chord with audiences.

*Disclosure* would be no different. Based on Michael Crichton's best-selling novel, it was the story of Meredith Johnson (Demi), the newly appointed executive at an electronics corporation who, during an office meeting after hours, sexually harasses office subordinate and old flame Tom Sanders (Michael Douglas) into picking up where they left off. It is where she sets the time, orders the wine, locks the door, demands service and loses her rag when she doesn't get it. She takes revenge for his rebuttal in dramatic style with a trumped-up charge of sexual assault, which in turn blocks any chance he might have of promotion within the company. But so confident is he that the charge won't stick, he even turns down the offer of a lateral move to another plant in Austin. Not only does he risk being rejected by his wife, family and colleagues, but he also stands to lose his job. The last straw comes when Meredith undercuts him by switching business strategies to make him appear incompetent. But the tables are turned when Sanders finally chooses to protect his honour with a lawsuit. Meredith's account, casting Sanders as the aggressor and herself as the victim, only confirms the suspicions of her defence. In the end, of course, Sanders is reinstated with compensation and Meredith is promptly given her marching orders.

Although Demi wasn't the first choice of director Barry Levinson, and had been recruited to fill the place of Annette Bening who had dropped out at the last minute, her association with the movie captured the imagination of American writers and, for that matter, the public. The story of Demi Moore – the tough cookie in charge of her own life as portrayed in three major articles in *Vanity Fair* – had a certain affinity with the character she was playing, at least from the standpoint of her single-minded approach to her career. Sexual harassment, of course, was not on Demi's personal agenda. She relied on straightforward strength of will. Tales from the set regurgitated her now-familiar demands for a double-sized trailer and a private plane to carry her to location filming in Seattle. But, then again, as she said herself, why not? Although Michael Douglas had the star treatment written into his $12 million contract, it still added a fresh angle for journalists visiting the set during filming (in accordance with Douglas's normal policy of an open set, he always welcomed pre-release publicity). Demi, on the other hand, they pointed out, was playing 'a woman who is capable of anything if it means she'll win' or 'a woman you'll love to hate'.

Moore was quick to dismiss the tattle, distancing herself from the character. 'I've met women like the one I'm playing. They see all men as fair game and they enjoy it that way. But that's not me, no way,' she said. 'Women are brought up to believe it's okay to have sex if your intention is to get married,' she elaborated. 'Men are told to get out there and screw as much as possible because you're a *maaaan*. The score is the thing. The [crux of] the role reversal in *Disclosure* is the awkwardness in that Tom Sanders is having to say, "I've been harassed," because culturally he's saying, "I'm being less of a man because I didn't go ahead and screw her." That occurred to me when some people started hinting, "Who's gonna really turn you down?" I couldn't believe how sexist that was, that what they were actually saying is that a man can't control himself if he's with a woman who may turn him on.'

Nowhere is that better expressed than in the sex scene she was called upon to play. 'For me, it's unique in itself. It isn't a love scene, it is purely just about sex and the nature of a woman who enjoys aggressive sex, and it's an integral part of the story. That scene working is what the whole of the rest of the movie feeds off. If that scene didn't work, the movie wouldn't have worked.'

All the same, she later admitted that when she watched the scene herself it embarrassed and even shocked her. 'I feel that I get a little silly. I just don't buy it, think I'm being camp. But Michael said it was easy for him because I did all the work. It was difficult, as all sex scenes are, but this one was made easier by the fact that we really choreographed it – more so than the other scenes I've had to do. Once I got the first take out the way, which scared the shit out of me, I went into a little room to kind of clean up and I asked the other women around me to give me some hot tips and then I went out and was much better.'

And that helped, she continues, because 'I think in the fantasy of the film, we want him to do it because he gets to live out what we don't do in real life. You know, "Please do it for us because we're not doing it at home. We have too much at stake. I may have had those thoughts, but do it for me and let me see how it goes." And so what they're doing is basing the question on fantasy, not reality.'

As before, Demi pushed herself through some rigorous and extensive workouts and punishing pre-dawn five-mile runs to ensure her post-pregnant body (after the birth of her youngest daughter, Tallulah Belle, whom she and Bruce named after Tallulah Bankhead, the flamboyant movie star of the 1930s and 1940s) was once more lithe and slender. Critics visiting the set were quick to point out that she was looking a million dollars. 'Not just any old million dollars either,' noted one. 'Crisp, freshly printed notes straight out of the cashpoint. With her hair hanging long and loose, she looks at first glance like – dare one say it – a schoolgirl. Not the least bit like the mean vixen who practically eats Michael Douglas for breakfast.'

*Disclosure* was released for Christmas 1994 in America and even though it may not have filled all the criteria for a seasonal movie, it rapidly became both a critical and box-office smash, eventually taking well in excess of $230 million in international receipts, and once again confirming Demi's ranking among the top actresses of the year. In box-office terms, at least, her films had now surpassed her husband's by almost half a billion* dollars.

The poster campaign for *Disclosure* showed Demi wrapped threateningly round a cornered Douglas with her dress yanked up high around her thighs, her hands placing his on her rear, and with the slogan 'Sex is Power' blazing out. How could the distributors, Warner Brothers, go wrong? The enforced chemistry, it seemed, had worked well. But it caused a storm of protest when the film was subsequently released in Britain and France and there were many demands that the graphic posters be removed from public display.

Within a few weeks of Bruce Willis announcing his $15 million fee to reprise the role of John McClane in the third of the *Die Hard* series, Demi made it public that she intended to follow *Disclosure* with the starring role in Roland Joffe's version of *The Scarlet Letter*. One naïve columnist, apparently familiar with Nathaniel Hawthorne's 1850 novel but less so with the inner workings of Hollywood, gave a lengthy explanation of Demi's suitability for the role: 'One can see at once why Joffe has selected her to take the lead in this movie.' What the journalist didn't realise was that Demi had chosen herself.

Keen to make a movie with some kind of serious statement, Demi had been mapping out the project since the early months of 1993, when she became determined to film a remake of the classic novel. She would earn a substantial guaranteed fee as the starring actor, plus a piece of the action on the rights.

* The reference to billion is the American term for one million million dollars and should not be confused with the British equivalent for a billion, namely 'one thousand million pounds'.

She knew that she faced a battle to get her movie made. It would never be considered anything more than mediocre box-office material by the financiers; even more courageously, as the star, she would be carrying the picture solely on her own merit. She claimed that didn't worry her: 'I never saw it as a star vehicle for me,' she said. 'It was never going to be a blockbuster, although obviously you don't set out to make a movie that loses money.'

Although the success of *Disclosure* ensured Demi's star was still shining brightly, the Hollywood powers-that-be and their backers were of the opinion that very few female stars could carry a movie on their own with anything approaching success. Nor could anyone visualise Demi decked out in period costume or wrapping her distinctive American accent around the plummy vowels of an Englishwoman.

Demi didn't share those doubts. From her offices off Sunset Boulevard, Suzanne Todd, president of Moving Pictures and producer of films such as *National Lampoon Loaded Weapon 1*, and David Willis were now in the final planning stages of *The Scarlet Letter*. As far as Demi was concerned she would still, despite her doubters, take the leading role of Hester Prynne, the married woman who scandalised puritanical seventeenth-century New England by having an illegitimate child. For refusing to name the father, she was adorned with a scarlet letter 'A' for adultery.

The project also offered her the chance to work with Andrew Vanja's Cinergi Productions. He was now on board as the film's co-producer and set about finding a studio to underwrite the $50 million needed to bankroll the movie. He found it with Disney's Buena Vista, who promptly picked up the American rights and ended up with a movie that would eventually gross just over a disappointing $10 million.

If developing the film proved arduous, casting was less complicated. Gary Oldman, who in the past had played the roles of Sid Vicious and Lee Harvey Oswald, and more recently at that time, Count Dracula in Francis Ford Coppola's breathtaking 1992 remake, was the correct choice for the role of Reverend Arthur Dimmesdale, Hester's lover and the father of her illegitimate child. Robert Duvall, a veteran of three Coppola movies, was recruited to play Hester's husband, Roger Prynne.

With finance and cast in place, Demi set out to find a suitable screenwriter to adapt Hawthorne's original tale, a tricky task if only because, as Demi remarked, it was 'a very dense, uncinematic book'. She eventually settled on Douglas Day Stewart. The difficulty facing them was how to make *The Scarlet Letter* work with twentieth-century implications.

Finding a director was easy: Roland Joffe was simply enthusiastic about the project. It probably helped that he, too, regarded the novel as a story of seventeenth-century morals and, like Demi, considered the film would have to demonstrate that the tale had indeed emerged from 'a time when the seeds were being sown for bigotry, sexism and lack of tolerance that we still battle today'. In other words, a morality tale with modern implications.

Although many would argue that great literature is sacred and should never be touched by Hollywood, there are examples of great books that have made great films. The idea of making another version of Hawthorne's classic was nevertheless still a gamble. One of America's most powerful novels, it was a book that had already spawned ten movies during the silent era, including its best loved incarnation in 1926 with Lillian Gish and Lars Hanson playing the roles now to be taken by Demi and Oldman.

Transferring the thoughts and inspirations from the minds of literary characters to the screen is notoriously difficult. Director Nicholas Hytner discovered much the same with his version of Arthur Miller's McCarthy-esque study of the Salem witch trails. Even then, with a screenplay by Miller himself, stars of the calibre of Daniel Day-Lewis and Winona Ryder and some rented hand-me down costumes from Demi's movie, Hytner could not turn *The Crucible* into a box-office smash either.

Outside of her own circle of colleagues, Demi was considered an odd choice for the part of Hester Prynne, even though she fitted the author's description perfectly: 'Her face was beautiful from regularity of feature and richness of complexion' is how Hawthorne described her. 'She has dark, abundant hair so glossy that it threw off sunshine like a beam.' It was seemingly what attracted Demi to the book in the first place. Now, more than ever, she was convinced she was right for the part. In retrospect, her fascination with Hester Prynne should not have been surprising. It has since proven characteristic of her favourite kind of role: independent, strong and intelligent.

All the same it was a far cry from any role she had played in the past, but she was not concerned. In fact, she leapt into the part, as much as she had with her pivotal role in the movie's creation. According to co-star Joan Plowright, who was recruited to play the freethinking Harriet Hibbons, she didn't intervene that much, although the Hollywood gossip mill insisted otherwise. Another rumour suggested that Plowright, one of Britain's finest actresses, and the widow of Laurence Olivier, working alongside a relatively untrained popular star with a prima donna reputation, might make for an interesting drama of goings-on behind the scenes. (Much the same was reported of

Gwyneth Paltrow and Judi Dench on the set of *Shakespeare in Love* some years later.) But Plowright insisted that Demi was 'very natural and very honest in seeking where she wants to go with a part. We were just two actresses at work. No nonsense. I must say that she behaved very well. She was very likeable. I saw none of that movie-star behaviour, although, of course, I'm sure she's capable of that.'

Demi's intention first and foremost was to 'make a movie that was as good as it could be'. Once again, it was one that she would disrobe for, and one for which she seemed quite happy for Joffe's camera to roam across her naked body while caressing herself. Aside from the sex, voyeurism, violence and happy ending, the scene was one of the themes Douglas Day Stewart considered necessary to develop further in his 1990s screenplay, since the novel begins *after* Hester's adultery has been committed.

A number of other inventions were also considered essential. The story would still centre around Hester, the young wife who arrives in puritanical New England minus her husband, who is feared dead, to begin her new life alone, staying in a cottage located on the edge of the community. Not long after her arrival she is strolling through the closely situated woodland when she happens upon Reverend Dimmesdale, the spiritual leader of the community, bathing naked in the water below.

In the novel, the author eloquently describes the lustful thoughts of the young woman as a result of being starved of love and attention. In the movie, they would reveal themselves more evidently, such as when Mituba, an attractive slave girl, played by Lisa Jolliff-Andoh, is introduced to prepare Hester's bath. Observing through a peephole, with interracial lesbian fascination, she watches her mistress caressing her lily-white naked body in soap while dreaming of the equally naked Reverend Dimmesdale. As critic Roger Ebert succinctly put it, the scene was treated as 'an additional thrill of one attractive woman observing another one naked'. Unfortunately, it was also cripplingly inappropriate, as was the second instance of Mituba's voyeurism: when the Reverend calls upon Hester to commit their sinful act on an uncomfortable bed of dried beans in the barn, the slave girl, now stripped off herself, climbs into her mistress's bath holding a lighted candle, and as the illicit love scene reaches its climax, she lets the candle sink beneath the water, extinguishing the flame with a hiss.

Not long after, Hester, now pregnant and refusing to reveal the name of her seducer, is compelled by the local bigots to wear a scarlet letter 'A' on her bodice. The drama heightens when her husband, Roger Prynne (Duvall), turns up, much to everyone's disbelief. He, of course, is shocked and furious to discover that his wife is now expecting a child. According to the novel, he had never had sex in his life, and didn't want anybody else to partake either. The rest of the movie concentrates on his desire for vengeance and his attempts to track down and scalp the father of his wife's illegitimate child. He murders the wrong man and then hangs himself in guilt. (Filming that particular scene nearly ended in real-life tragedy. The harness supporting Duvall snapped, almost killing the actor in the process, while the cameras were still rolling.)

The greatest difference between the novel and the movie, however, was the conclusion. Hawthorne's book ends with Dimmesdale confessing his sins on his deathbed, while in the film he transforms himself from despicable scoundrel into romantic hero – a campaigner, of all things, for religious toler-

As far as Demi was concerned, filming *Indecent Proposal* with Robert Redford in August 1992 was a crucial development to her career – in terms of both salary and her star status.

Demi at the opening of Planet Hollywood at Walt Disney World in Orlando with shareholding partners Arnold Schwarzenegger, Bruce Willis and Sylvester Stallone.

Demi and Bruce in 1995, then still Hollywood's most formidable pairing, at Planet Hollywood in San Diego.

After performing a song at a
Planet Hollywood opening
with husband Bruce Willis,
Demi said: 'People can't bear
the idea that we could create
a wonderful life together.'

Demi happily holds the
People's Choice award she
won for her nomination as
Favourite Dramatic Motion
Picture Actress in 1993.

In *Striptease* (1996), Demi and
Rumer, then 7, play
mother–daughter roles that
director Andrew Bergman felt
would bring their on-screen
relationship a level of reality.

Demi proudly received the
Female Star of the Year
award from the National
Association of Theater
Owners at a movie event in
Las Vegas, March 1994.

**TOP:** Just one week before *Passion of Mind* hit US screens in July 2000, Demi announced she was taking time out from making movies to spend with her three daughters, Rumer, Scout and Tallulah Belle – shown here on a Los Angeles beach.

**ABOVE:** Although Demi denied 'kissing and making out' with her psychic, Laura Day is shown here in seemingly affectionate mood.

RIGHT: Demi won her second Golden Globe nomination – this time for Best Performance in a Mini-series or Motion Picture Made for Television – for her portrayal of a nurse with an unwanted pregnancy in *If These Wall Could Talk*.

BELOW: The bizarre rumour that Demi had been living a secret lesbian life probably wasn't helped by her smooching lesbian actress and her *Juror* co-star Anne Heche at the Emmy Awards in Sepetember 1997.

Demi, an avid patron of the arts, is shown here arriving to
substitute for Elizabeth Taylor at the Cinema Against AIDS
event during the Cannes Film Festival in May 1997.

Demi's arrival (without Bruce Willis) at a private cocktail party on the eve of the Oscars in March 1998 publicly revealed what the Hollywood grapevine had speculated for months - that she and Willis had finally called it quits.

Following her break-up with Bruce Willis, Demi was spotted frequently shopping in Idaho: she is shown here in April 1999.

After a two-year absence from the screen, Demi joined the set of Alain Berliner's *Passion of Mind* on 29 September 1999 and is shown here on location in New York.

HOLLYWOOD
OLL
OLL
OLI
OLL
W
WO
D
OLLYWOOD HOLLYWO

Playing dual roles in *Passion of Mind* promised to give Demi's film career a much-needed boost, even though the script had been doing the Hollywood rounds for almost a decade. She is shown here on location in New York with co-star William Fichtner.

ance and sexual freedom. Even when the villagers are about to hang Hester for her stubborn silence, Dimmesdale, now accepting that he may have sinned, grasps the rope and pulls it around his own neck, only to be saved from death by an attacking tribe of savage Indians.

Although purists and historians would probably argue that the revisionist finale reduced the impact and changed what the story was all about, Demi was adamant her version had merit. 'In truth, it has been a very long time since most people have read it,' she told *Premiere* magazine. 'So if they get caught up in the notion that this film is some kind of a betrayal of classic literature, it's never going to work for them. If you watch the movie, just for the movie's sake, it works. It's not total happily-ever-after.' After watching the rough cut, she was even more convinced: 'I really think there's a movie there.'

Even today, she remains bold about the decision. 'I proposed that Dimmesdale shouldn't die,' she said. 'I pushed strongly for that, and Roland Joffe made a conscious decision, and we as the actors accepted his decision. But because of [all the fuss about the ending], no one looked at the film's merit. And in the end, Joffe realised that he should have had Dimmesdale die, and actually, in the final hour, he wanted to reshoot the ending. But we were so far down the line by then it was just logistically and financially impossible. It was just too late.'

Even if Joffe had had a change of heart, he probably felt no reservations about the way the film eventually turned out. Besides, working with Demi made up for any disappointment. 'There were times when she used to laugh,' he recalled fondly. 'I've kept some of the out-takes. Something would go wrong in a scene, and this laugh was absolutely enchanting. It's the real

Demi: completely open and vulnerable. But sometimes I would catch this edge of a very deep sadness as well. And that comes out of childhood. My God, she didn't choose any of those things she went through. Her victory is that she's come through all that. And that has the possibility of its own happy ending.'

He elaborates: 'Often people who have one parent that committed suicide, or come from an unhappy home, will flit between two extremes: extraordinary sociableness and complete closure. They have days when they think they're wonderful, and that makes them very open; or they go through a day when their self-esteem is low, and that makes them sharp and angry. That would be my observation of Demi, whom I love very much. In me, that bred a great tenderness towards her.'

Bruce Willis made the cross-country trek to the set of *The Scarlet Letter* as often as he could. Throughout the filming of the third and final *Die Hard*, he travelled back and forth to see Demi at weekends and whenever he could find a break in his shooting schedule. For the tabloid press, of course, this didn't matter. Their relationship was still worthy news, and any unsubstantiated rumour of a break-up would only spice up the gossip.

In attempting to add a twentieth-century message to the movie, the emotion of guilt, so crucial in Hawthorne's novel, virtually disappeared. Nevertheless, *The Scarlet Letter* offered some good performances, especially from Moore, Oldman and Duvall, who were as convincing as the material would allow. But the novel, which had proved itself so often to be beyond the powers of Hollywood in the past, was not, according to the first reviews that rolled in following its October 1995 release, satisfactorily dealt with this time either. One aim had been achieved, however: Demi had again been assured her upward rise would continue.

She and Bruce were now once again developing their multi-million-dollar earning potential. With their movies and production companies, the Planet Hollywood chain and their growing portfolio of real-estate and property, their fortunes could only improve. Their production companies were developing more than a couple of dozen possible future projects between them, not necessarily all as vehicles for themselves. Demi's most successful to date have been the two Austin Powers movies: *International Man of Mystery* and *The Spy Who Shagged Me*. Like Bruce, she too took out options on the movie rights to books, scripts and screenplays.

Both partners were treading cautiously in that Hollywood deal-making minefield which so many stars try to negotiate, with varying degrees of success, in an attempt to gain control of their own destiny. Some get involved behind the scenes for the art and to further their careers. Others do it simply to get their hands on the box-office coffers and on the international rights, television deals, videos, soundtrack albums and other merchandising products that are all now part and parcel of the bigger movies. Willis had made his opinions on that subject quite clear. He and Demi – and she, especially, on the movie production side – wanted to build on their activities as film-makers as well as actors. They were also diversifying strongly into other areas. By the end of 1995, their respective positioning in the industry had undergone rapid and remarkable consolidation. Bruce in particular had come from a point in 1993 where his career was definitely on the skids to a position of considerable strength and renewed power. He was also beginning to get something he had yearned after for years: respect.

With their joint millions, their financial status could never be described as precarious, and even though the world in which they circulated certainly had enough sharks, they were astute enough to build upon strong foundations to ensure their capital would not simply drift away. They weren't short of money, but did they blow it on wild excesses? They would most probably have to furrow their brows to try to remember. They did have huge outgoings, however, in tax, agents, managers, their three homes and a vast personal staff. However, the possibility of it all ending tomorrow – in terms of star status at least – had been virtually eliminated with their recent outings on the silver screen.

In the preceding eighteen months they had between them bolstered their bank balances by well in excess of $50 million. Although the basic art of movie-making still got a look in from time to time, somewhere along the line in the deal-making machinery, finance had become the predominant feature. It was in this respect that the mid-1990s witnessed a considerable expansion in taking care of business as the money settled around this now 'truly golden couple' in ever increasing circles.

Although the couple had already been ploughing money – an estimated $8 million, according to some sources – into property in their adopted hometown of Hailey, in Sun Valley, it was not until the spring of 1995 that they would focus their attentions on their latest acquisition. The town's old art deco cinema, the Liberty, was facing hard times after a new four-screen theatre had opened in nearby Ketchum. The Liberty, which first opened in 1938, was a grim, rundown box of a place with peeling paint-work, broken seats, no screen curtains and an old projection system that often broke down. The Willises bought it at a knock-down price and began a stylish refurbishment.

Demi placed herself in charge of the décor, hiring the services of interior designer Colin Cowie. Between them, they came up with a thorough revamp: the new interiors of gilt and glass fitted the building's original era, and rich colour schemes of burgundy and bronze ran through the interior, with matching velvet curtains hung around the screen. Bruce shipped in $150,000 worth of new electronics and state-of-the-art sound systems as well as two new projectors. One would show the latest releases and the other would be used to screen old classics and Saturday-morning movies for kids. With the refit complete, they organised a grand reopening with a hometown première of Willis's latest movie, *Twelve Monkeys*.

Although the cinema revamp was probably nothing more than another piece of redevelopment in Hailey to Bruce and Demi, it still managed to raise the eyebrows of the locals. Was this nostalgic self-indulgence or true business sense? The couple's motives for acquiring five major properties on Main Street was never quite clear to the townspeople. Across the street from the cinema, they had already started building a planned museum to house Demi's collection of dolls and Bruce's vintage motorcycles.

Both were also still involved with Planet Hollywood. In the four years since the company was founded, it had grown enormously and now consisted of twenty-four company-owned outlets and six franchises in nine countries across North America, Europe and Asia. Now, in 1995, it had extended the concept to two other theme chains: the Official All Star Café (sports-based restaurants/merchandise shops) and Marvel Mania (comic-book-themed restaurants and shops) and was attracting many other celebrities as sponsors.

The company expected to have a total of 51 restaurant and merchandise stores set up, in 16 different countries, by the end of 1996, including 45 under the Planet Hollywood logo. In its accounts for 1995 it could boast total revenues of over $270 million. That extraordinary figure was expected to double within two years, and be heading well beyond $1 billion per annum by the start of the millennium.

One of the co-founders, Robert Earl, with a 28.8 per cent stake at the time he prepared it for public flotation, had become one of Britain's wealthiest businessmen. Bruce and Demi, as members of the original small group of celebrities who were granted share options, remained among the largest stakeholders. Some 17 per cent of the company was jointly owned by the celebrity group. They were quietly delighted when the company was floated in the early months of 1996 on New York's Nasdaq market. Shares rocketed from the $18 issue price to $25, giving the company a value of $2.7 billion – and making the celebrities' stake close to half a billion.

Bruce and Demi and the other shareholders were also hoping to reap the massive financial benefits as Earl proceeded with his publicly announced plans to turn the company into a $20 billion global empire to challenge the likes of Disney and Time Warner. 'I want to create the largest and most successful leisure company in the world,' he said expansively after the flotation launch of Planet Hollywood. In his 25 years in the business, Earl has an enviable record of success, including the foundation of the Hard Rock Café chain, now owned by Britain's Rank Organisation. By the mid-1990s Planet Hollywood, with its star turns and support, had become his most successful venture to date. His plans for the future included themed music and live entertainment restaurants, along with superstores which would sell a thousand-item range of Planet Hollywood merchandise. It was hardly surprising that Bruce and Demi participated so willingly in the cause – hyping the company for all its worth at every opportunity.

Some observers noted at the time that if Earl did succeed in his ambition to turn Planet Hollywood into the leisure mammoth he believed it was destined to become, the Willises would be sitting on top of a goldmine worth something approaching a billion dollars, regardless of what they stood to make from movies.

# TO DISNEY
# WITH LOVE

*'When I was younger I didn't have a lot of self-esteem.
Somebody I knew told me that I've changed more than any
person he's ever met. I take that as a really nice compliment'*

DEMI MOORE

As if to prove that she was unstoppable, Demi's next role was confirmed just as she was wrapping up work on *The Scarlet Letter*. It had been proposed long before that, actually. Even during the shooting of Roland Joffe's film, Demi was rarely off the phone in between takes as she juggled projects in development with her demanding filming schedule. 'I had to take meetings while I was shooting,' she recalled. 'There was no other way to keep up. There were just five days between finishing *Disclosure* and starting *The Scarlet Letter* and, even then, I had no days off.'

Although Demi should probably have taken a break, she and Suzanne Todd, her partner at Moving Pictures, had already committed themselves to filming *The Gaslight Addition*. This movie, for release by New Line Cinema, was already in production when Demi arrived on set, and one that would eventually gross a moderate (by Hollywood standards) $27 million.

As she had done with *The Scarlet Letter*, Demi again took the dual roles of producer and co-star. As before, she insisted upon overall artistic control. And why not? 'Producing for me is a very natural experience,' she stated. 'Motherhood was the perfect training ground to be the problem-solver, because that's what you do all day. As a producer, I can't help but want to just nurture. It's also a creative outlet for me. I look for movies to make that educate me and teach me something new about myself. In the early part of my career, I had access only to material other people were developing. I felt powerless. Now I can make movies that interest me and might do things for other women.'

She wanted to keep the budget low, so she could end up with a film that was sure to strike a profitable chord with audiences. 'We found the script, we nurtured it, we cast it, and we hired a director. We were able to take it from the beginning to the end, and it was great fun.'

With its original title now changed to the snappier *Now and Then*, the film tells the story of four girls from a small town who in their youth make a pledge always to be there for one another. Twenty-five years after the summer they all turned twelve, a time comes when they do really need each other. Christina, played by Rita Wilson, is pregnant, and needs the support of her friends: gynaecologist Roberta (Rosie O'Donnell), Samantha (Demi Moore), now a successful novelist, and Teeny (Melanie Griffith), an equally famous actress. Together they reminisce about their childhood, as their juvenile counterparts, Ashleigh Aston Moore, Christina Ricci, Gaby Hoffman and Thora Birch respectively, take over their characters for more or less the rest of the movie.

This was something critic Roger Ebert couldn't understand: 'What was the purpose of the wraparound bookends with the adult stars whom we scarcely see again until the end?' he wondered. 'Although the screenplay isn't much help, the adult actresses are completely superfluous to the movie, and the four young wonderfully talented actresses would have been completely capable of filling the screen time without the adults' guest appearances. In theory we might be interested in seeing what kind of women the girls grew up to be, but the movie gives the adults so little screen time that it has to resort to shorthand, like using smoking as a character trait.'

The world in which their adolescence takes place is typical of 1970s America, where the four girls have pooled their money to buy a tree house. It's from here that their imaginary lives are hyperactively led by Samantha as they venture, among other things, into the cemetery one night for a candlelight seance, and develop a fascination for 'Dear Johnny' – a boy who died young in the 1940s. They want to know how, why and when.

It is also the summer they share secrets, communicate by walkie-talkie, ride to the nearest county town on their bicycles to look through back issues of the paper for clues about 'Dear Johnny', and wear bras for the first time. While Roberta, the tomboy of the group, tries taping her budding breasts down, Teeny, the future actress, yearns for bigger ones, stuffing her bra with bags of vanilla pudding. Needless to say, they also deal with boys, especially the hated Wormers, a gang of brothers who make their lives a misery. In one scene, almost obligatory in stories such as this, they steal the Wormers' clothes down at the old swimming hole, and even get a glimpse of at least one Wormer penis.

Adding an element of fright is a recluse named Crazy Pete who stalks the streets at night. He saves one of the girls from a raging storm after she loses her bracelet down a flooding sewer and climbs down to fetch it, almost drowning in the process.

While the critics were swift to dub it 'a contrived *Stand By Me* kind of story', others considered that *Now and Then* fell into what Hollywood observers euphemistically styled 'women's movies'. Roger Ebert called it 'a gimmicky sitcom made of artificial bits and pieces'. Not every review was so negative, but audiences were scarcely overwhelmed by the film's desperate attempts to create tension. Most credited Christina Ricci as the true star, and remarked how she stole every scene from her co-stars. She had received equally high praise for her previous roles in the likes of *Mermaids*, *Casper* and *The Addams Family*.

The indifferent reviews had little effect on the film's director, Leslie Linka Glatter. In the press notes, she confessed to weeping when she first read the script because it captured that 'delicate evolution from girlhood to womanhood, and you so rarely find that'. It did not strike the same chord at the box office. It was further evidence, if any were needed, that Demi, like her husband in the early days, was prepared to take on lesser projects for her own personal satisfaction. She appeared to be concentrating on the market for smaller movies which, like *Ghost*, might just succeed and take the Hollywood high-rollers by surprise. Demi, to her credit, was prepared to tackle projects that fell into that category, seemingly without fear of any negative effects on her own acting career. This was something she reinforced when she talked to a reporter from Britain's *Film Review*. 'I wanted to make *Now and Then* because it's a story about four young girls. I got a lot of strong feedback from women who were excited that there was a project for other women out there, especially one geared towards young women. I myself never lived in the same home longer than six months while I was growing up, so I never had the opportunity to have the kind of friendships [portrayed in the film]. I guess I sort of only had an idea of what it must have been like. Also, it was interesting for me in that it dealt with life's betrayals and the loss of innocence. The material was charming, funny, sweet and endearing.'

Demi relished the opportunity to work alongside a director making her feature film début, and with a cast and crew that was predominantly female in all the major creative roles. 'It's important to me,' she made clear, 'that women in this business be successful, and it's nice to be able to give them their breaks in a male-orientated industry. A lot of men visited the set and asked, "Where are the men?" It felt good to have so many women on a set, because usually most of the people on crews are guys,' she remembered with a laugh.

Directly after completing *Now and Then*, Demi found herself on the set of her next movie, *The Juror*. She had read the manuscript of George Dawes Green's book long before she saw the movie script, and she knew instinctively that she wanted the part of the main character. Annie Laird, a single mother and struggling sculptor, eagerly volunteers to serve on the jury in the trial of a Mafia godfather accused of murder. 'She's at a point in her life where she's a little bored and looking for a distraction,' Demi explained. 'Being a juror doesn't seem to be harmful and it will momentarily take her out of what she perceives as her humdrum life, but she also wants to set an example to her son about being responsible and serving your country.'

During the jury selection process, however, Annie is evaluated not only by the judge and attorneys, but also by a Mafia hit-man known as the Teacher, played by Alec Baldwin. 'He is very adept at electronics and surveillance methods,' Baldwin said of his character, 'and he's been hired by the mob to help them select someone in the jury, someone they can use to allow them to tamper with the jury's verdict.' He has already copied pictures, taken phone numbers and set up transmitter bugs inside Annie's home to allow him to know her every move. He enters her life under the guise of Mark Cordell, supposedly an art buyer, who has bought several of her sculptures for a staggering $24,000. She can hardly believe her luck.

It is not long before the threats begin when he comes clean about his intention to kill her and her son unless she can persuade the jury to return a verdict of not guilty on the Mafioso. Not even Annie's best friend, Juliet (Anne Heche), is safe. In fact, when the Teacher murders her, Annie realises she has no option but to go along with his plan. But how can she persuade the others to share her point of view when she doesn't believe it herself? Annie becomes the Teacher's primary student, his obsession and his love. But she is absolutely trapped.

The project appealed to Demi because: 'I think our instinct is to believe that our judicial system is pure and honourable and will protect us, but the Teacher teaches Annie that this isn't always true.' She went on: 'They really become teacher and pupil. He pushes her to find the strength and passion to turn the jury around, and he derives great pleasure out of seeing her transformed into the strong personality that he knew existed within her all along. The chess game really begins when she steps outside the boundaries that he has set and takes action on her own.'

The climax of the movie centres around Annie's battle to stop the Teacher's attempt to kill her son, which in turn leads to a shoot-out in, of all places, the jungles of Guatemala. Echoing Sally Field's *Eye for an Eye* of the previous year, in that final scene of Annie standing over her dead aggressor, gun still smoking from the half-dozen rounds she's blasted him with, and now reunited with her son, she is the very image of someone breaking out of her own worst nightmare.

This was something that intrigued the film's director, Brian Gibson (best known at the time for the 1993 Tina Turner biopic *What's Love Got to With It*). 'I am very interested in the idea that one cannot escape one's destiny,' he explained. In the film, 'the Teacher cannot commit all these evil acts and not be revisited one day by what he has done. I was really interested in this concept of justice – not just the justice that does or does not happen in the courtroom, but a kind of justice that looms larger than that.'

He analysed the character of Annie as a woman who 'has been seduced into co-operating with this man by his flattery of her art, and by believing that she's possibly falling in love with some-body. So, when he reveals to her the real reason for his interest in her, there's a deep violation which echoes what happens to the rape victim who doesn't go to the police afterwards because the humiliation of what has been done to them is too private and too personal to reveal to anybody.'

That invasion of privacy is what Demi related to in Annie, especially the scene where the Teacher reveals his true interest in her: 'It's a terrible betrayal.' She explained further: 'Here is a woman who hasn't wanted to open herself up to be vulnerable with a man and then finds somebody she's attracted to, opens herself up and is completely devastated to learn that he's really there for some other reason entirely. It becomes the beginning of a ride of absolute torment and terror.'

Most of *The Juror*'s punch is delivered in the second half of the film. Abruptly shifting its emphasis midway through, when the boot is firmly placed on the other foot, the stronger and more determined Annie sets out to trap the Teacher, and the hunted becomes the hunter.

Talking about how he brought *The Juror* to the screen, the film's producer, Irwin Winkler (of Sylvester Stallone's five *Rocky* movies), revealed that he 'had been lucky enough to serve on a jury in Los Angeles. I was fascinated by the functioning of the jury system, intrigued by the whole process. And I had read an article in the *New Yorker* about a newspaper reporter who had served on a jury in New York, which had got my interest but I decided there wasn't enough of a drama to it. Then an agent who knew I was interested in the subject sent me over a manuscript of Dawes's book. I read it overnight and bought it [the film rights] the next day.'

Tom Hutchinson, writing in *Film Review*, observed that the movie has 'almost certainly the best ever performances by Demi Moore and Alec Baldwin'. Even so, he had to admit *The Juror* was flawed: 'Its plot has had the unfortunate fate of having been dealt from the bottom of the believe-it-or-not deck. It is one of those movies which could quite easily have been aborted early in the drama if the terrorised victim had just done the obvious thing and reached for the phone to call the cops.' All the same, he did agree with other reviewers, 'that the ability of Baldwin and Moore to make the bizarre characters far more believable than the story itself is a measure of their growing star status. They almost make up for the deficiencies of structure and the violent predictability of the movie's outcome.'

Demi was given precious little time to absorb any of the reviews as, once again, she barely had any time off in between movies. Even when she did find a break in her schedule she still filled it with work, work, work. She did, however, find sufficient time to pose topless for *George* magazine, John F. Kennedy Jnr's political lifestyle rag, whose every issue featured a celebrity on the cover dressed as the American President. For Demi, of course, there was a twist: she would be decked out as the First Lady, Martha Washington – and, according to Mr Showbiz on the internet, she wore nothing but a hoop skirt; over her bare breasts (painted in a conscious echo of *Vanity Fair*) were the constitutional colours of the Stars and Stripes.

At the same time, she was also 'starring' in Disney's animated version of *The Hunchback of Notre Dame*. She was the voice of Esmeralda, the female lead. Released in June 1996, the film remains among the best loved of all Disney's cartoon features.

Based loosely on the classic French horror tale by Victor Hugo, *The Hunchback of Notre Dame* is set in fifteenth-century Paris. Clopin the puppeteer tells the story of Quasimodo, the disfigured but gentle bell ringer of Notre Dame cathedral who, as an infant, was almost slaughtered by Claude Frollo, the Minister of Justice. But Frollo was ordered by the Archdeacon to raise the misshapen child as if he were his own. Now a young man, Quasimodo is hidden away from the world by Frollo in the bell tower of the cathedral. It's only during the Festival of Fools that, cheered on by his sole friends, Victor, Hugo and Laverne (the cathedral's stone gargoyles), Quasimodo participates in the festivities. Something goes wrong and he has to be rescued from the raging crowds by gypsy girl Esmeralda, dark-haired, wide-eyed, vivacious and beautiful – Demi herself to all intents and purposes – and the out-of-favour captain of Frollo's troops, Phoebus. In no time at all, the three of them are ranged against the evil Frollo's outrageous efforts to destroy the Court of Miracles – the home of the gypsies. The rest of the movie centres on Quasimodo's desperate attempt to defend the cathedral and Esmeralda, with whom he has now fallen head over heels in love.

In one memorable review, critic Roger Ebert summed up the general critical opinion when he credited the film 'a whirling, uplifting, thrilling story with a heart-touching message – that there is room in the world for many different kinds of people, for hunchbacks and gypsies as well as for those who scornfully consider themselves the norm – emerges from the comedy and song'. But *Empire*'s Hannah Whitlow remarked that 'not even her one-dimensional alter-ego could escape the stereotype. Esmeralda, Demi's cartoon counterpart, challenged the boundaries of Disney animators: here was the Little Mermaid with breasts! Belle with better moves! Pocahontas with more cleavage! In fact, Esmeralda was downright racy, even entertaining her fellow poverty-stricken peasants with, of all things, a pole dance.'

Demi, strangely enough, was unconcerned, despite all her previous attempts to control her public image. But maybe that was down to the fact that the real-life equivalent of the character her voice portrayed on the screen was not the real her. 'I really don't know what people think my image is, but I know what I'm about. I feel clear within myself, and where I come from, and what my intentions are. Ultimately, people have a right to their opinions and perceptions. It's not anything that I have control over, or have the right to hold an opinion on.'

Talking about her role in the animated classic, Demi revealed that 'as a contemporary art collector, I know how faces are created. With animation the eyes are always very large with a small chin. They video you when you do your voiceover so I saw my expressions. You do see yourself. Esmeralda doesn't look exactly like me. She actually has black skin but I am *so* there. Even when I had to take my kids to see *Toy Story* for the tenth time and they were showing the trailer, it was so odd to look and hear my voice because it didn't even seem like me for a moment.'

She lent her voice to another animated feature six months later, though far less prominently this time. She and Bruce contributed to Mike Judge's *Beavis and Butthead Do America*. Neither cameo 'appearance' was listed in the credits, however. According to Judge, their agents demanded the actors' parts remain anonymous, considering their salary didn't amount to much. Neither could he use their names in connection to the movie's promotion.

Around this time – just like Beavis and Butthead, in fact – Demi had returned to the medium through which she had entered Hollywood in the first place. Early in her career, she had commented upon the impact of television on popular culture and taste, and was now back on the small screen to prove it. She had a good reason this time. Her entry into the debate about abortion – a subject that no Hollywood studio would touch – must rank among the most courageous decisions she has ever made. Getting involved in making a film about such an emotive topic could have had severely detrimental effects on her career in a country like America where feelings on both sides of the argument often spill over into violence.

*If These Walls Could Talk*, the emotional stories of three women with unwanted pregnancies in the second half of the twentieth century, had endured a slow gestation in development. Demi herself had first discussed the project with her Moving Pictures partner Suzanne Todd in the early 1990s. Four years later, established and confident in their respective fields of production, their passion for the idea remained undimmed.

It was much the same for Colin Callender, then senior vice-president at HBO, one of America's premier cable channels. For as long as he could remember, he, too, had the idea of making a movie about abortion. It wasn't until now that he had found a script that could do the topic justice. The other difficulty facing such a project was his accurate assumption that 'I don't believe there was a studio in the world that would have financed this picture.'

But the story 'wasn't specifically pro-choice', Demi explained. 'We tried to make it reflect both sides of the issue, regardless of what our personal views are, and in that way allow people to make their own decision. If it happens to have an impact on people on a bigger level, that would be wonderful!'

Above all else, she continued, 'We were striving to communicate the importance of the personal issues. We wanted to take abortion out of the political arena . . . Whether or not abortion is illegal, inside the woman it is still painful, it's still difficult. It takes a lot of courage to make either decision.'

The movie was divided into three segments, one for each of the decades – the 1950s, 1970s and 1990s – named in Pamela and Earl Wallace's screenplay. Demi's part was set in 1952 where, as Nurse Claire Donnelly, widowed by the Korean War, she struggles to keep up with payments on the house she acquired in better times. She lives in a society that frowns on anyone who is divorced. One can only imagine, then, the horror she must feel when she discovers that she is pregnant from a brief and complicated liaison in the arms of her brother-in-law when she was looking for consolation.

Although Claire knows she cannot keep the unborn child, the law forbids her to have an abortion. Despite her profession, her appeal for help from a doctor is greeted with nothing more than condescension and scorn. Claire's desperate appeal for assistance from those closest to her is rebuffed with the accusation that she has shamed the family. After taking matters into her own hands, and attempting unsuccessfully to perform the abortion herself with a knitting needle, she finds momentary relief when a doctor is willing to make a house call. But he is only interested in the money, and bothers neither to sterilise his instruments for the eventual kitchen-table operation, nor about the bleeding woman he leaves behind.

The segment was shot with director Nancy Savoca and a regular crew that February. Savoca, interestingly enough, would be Demi's second female director, and the actress knew it would again be a very different experience from what she had undergone in the past. 'We've only worked together one day so far, and it's been great,' she smiled on set. '[Savoca's] whole relationship with the camera is different. I don't mean to say that it's better or worse, but there is something very different between what men and women do with the camera. I think it's a kind of feminism. I wish I had a chance to work with more women on the sets.'

The director of the third segment, set in 1996, was Cher. Like Demi an executive producer on the project, she was making her début behind the camera as well as starring in the film. 'It took someone of Demi's power and fortitude to have something like this made,' she stated. 'Without that power we couldn't have done this because these issues – which are considered "women's issues" – are not on everyone's top ten list of things to do.'

Cher, needless to say, was perfect for this project. Since she had broken up with her husband Sonny Bono, she had single-mindedly established herself among America's top rock'n'rollers. Having already carved out a successful Hollywood career with the likes of *Silkwood*, *Mask*, *The Witches of Eastwick*, *Suspect* and *Mermaids*, no one doubted that her abilities would give even more momentum to the film.

When *If These Walls Could Talk* was first broadcast in America, on 13 October 1996 on the HBO cable channel following its première at the Toronto Film Festival, it rapidly became a smash in terms of both the ratings and the critics' response. 'The movie network's decision to air this film deserves nothing less than a standing ovation,' raved the *Toronto Sun*'s Claire Bickley. 'No mainstream broadcaster would have touched this uncompromising and sometimes grisly movie.' Hers was only one of many enthusiastic reviews. She continued: '*Walls* never cops out, never glosses over, never pulls a punch. But it does have a point of view and it does take a side – the side of the women whose stories it tells – no matter what decision they make about their pregnancies. The point is that whatever the era, whatever the political climate, abortion has always been, and always should be, one woman's personal decision.'

For Demi, emerging at last from the critical darkness that had consumed so much of her career, the additional acclaim of her peers – a nomination for Best Performance in a Mini-series or Motion Picture Made for Television at the 1997 Golden Globes ceremony – was the icing on the cake.

# PICTURE NOT
# SO PERFECT

*'Everyone has a right to one or two or even three flops.*
*It's a gamble every time you have a movie out there.*
*Even when you have the best director and the best*
*actors, you never know if the audience will come'*

DEMI MOORE

Demi Moore tells her assistant to put on Annie Lennox, track six. The music starts. She pulls off her shirt and trousers, lets her hair down and begins dancing in front of a full-length mirror. She wraps her index fingers around the strings of her white bikini underwear and pulls them up seductively as she gyrates round and round and round. Her hair flies. Her breasts sway in her black bra. If anyone had any doubts about her next role, in Andrew Bergman's *Striptease*, they shouldn't have been concerned. Demi wasn't.

Her three previous movies could hardly be considered major hits in terms of either box-office receipts or their reception by the critics, and the Hollywood rumour mill went into overdrive with suggestions that there was much more than money resting upon the success of *Striptease*.

Certain announcements made long before filming even began probably did nothing to diffuse the situation. The news that Demi would be paid $12.5 million for her role – making her the highest paid actress of her time – for what initially seemed like an excuse to take her kit off again, this time as a strip artist, had most of Hollywood shocked, bemused or furious. She shrugged off the reaction: 'It feels good to be paid twelve and a half million dollars,' she would later state. 'Other actresses' pay jumped as a result of my fee. I'm very proud it has made a big difference for every woman in Hollywood.'

Despite such comments, there were those who remained incredulous. One was Hollywood columnist Martin Grove. He was quick to note that the movie 'had to work otherwise Demi may have to get a day job at Planet Hollywood. It's hard to justify that sort of money when you're not packing them in, and lately she hasn't been.' But he also admitted that if anyone could make it work, Demi Moore could.

Director Andrew Bergman and producer Mike Lobell were well aware of this. Demi was their first and only choice for the role of the film's main character, Erin Grant. 'Not only is Demi beautiful like Erin, but she also had the courage and confidence to play this role. And like Erin, Demi is straightforward, determined and resourceful. She has faced a lot of adversity in her own life, and has managed, by her pluck and strength of will, to overcome it,' Bergman said.

Demi, too, could not help but be aware of the implications of commercial failure, the mounting criticism and the amazement concerning her fee. The movie would prove both a challenge and a threat at the same time, and this is how she approached it: challenging, because there was probably no other female star on the Hollywood A-list who would have taken it on; and threatening not only because of the risk of flopping at the box office but also because of the nature of the film's nude scenes done for the voyeuristic benefit of the camera and the audience. As one observer astutely noted, though, she had already disrobed in six of her previous movies, and had appeared naked more than once on the cover of *Vanity Fair*. There wasn't much left of Demi Moore that the cinema-going public hadn't already seen.

It wasn't quite as simple as that, of course. The film centred on strip clubs and stripping, and Demi, by her own admission, knew little enough about that particular subject. Nevertheless, she leapt at the opportunity to play the lead role. Maybe that is what surprised people. She was, after all, best known for her cool, hard-as-nails portrayals of the modern woman, and was often seen as more feminist than feminine. This is partly why many considered her enthusiasm for the part rather odd. The actress herself accepted the role without hesitation, though, and her usual tough approach and determination got her through some of the film's most demanding sequences.

The actress said she was attracted to the role for a number of reasons: 'The story is grounded in a beautiful relationship between a mother and her daughter,' she explained. 'It's supported by a very action-orientated, interesting political agenda and unconventional characters. And the humour that's derived from all of that makes for an entertaining film. That's not to say people won't enjoy seeing the women dance. I enjoy the women dancing. And why can't we appreciate that as opposed to judging it as something wrong the way so many people do?'

It was not an easy role for her to prepare for. To play the part of Erin successfully she had to bond not only emotionally but also physically and intellectually with her character. This she did. Marguerite Derricks, a choreographer, was recruited to take her through her paces, but the actress insisted on getting some real-life experience of the world she was attempting to portray. She visited a number of strip clubs to consult real strippers. 'I found that a lot of these places are upmarket, and cater to businessmen and women. I think the bars have become more a place of enter-tainment rather than sleazy dives, which was my original percep-tion of them.'

She learned a great deal more than eroticism from her talks with the women she met there. At one club, the very first she went into, 'one of the strippers said to me, "Just remember one thing: always dance for yourself. Because if you don't, it will be for nothing." And what I realised when I started to practise by myself and focus on myself is that women are encouraged to be disconnected from the waist down. This kind of dancing encour-ages you to touch yourself, and to really get in touch with your own sensuality and what makes you feel good. That's where the confidence comes in. It's not about how you look; it's about how you feel. That's why I think every woman at some point should take time to go and stand in front of a mirror by herself and just move and dance in that way. There's something really empower-ing about it.'

Asked whether she had ever been attracted to a woman, Demi was quick to reply: 'I think women are beautiful, but it's a tough thing to get into. It's interesting, because I was asking one of the strippers what percentage of them are gay or bisexual, and she said, "I don't like to place gender on love." And I thought that was an amazing place to be in.' The fact that she was photographed smooching her *Juror* co-star Anne Heche at the Emmy awards ceremony that September while Bruce Willis did much the same with Heche's girlfriend Ellen DeGeneres doesn't seem to matter. Neither did, according to the *National Enquirer*, the time she allegedly fondled female journalist Diane Sawyer during an interview. On another occasion she denied 'kissing and making out' with her psychic advisor Laura Day.

Carl Hiaasen, the author of the novel on which *Striptease* was based, was surprised and impressed by Demi's work method. She had obviously read his book from cover to cover and then 'struck out with a journalistic appetite researching the stripping business'.

As filming began, so did Demi's now familiar routine of fitness and mind exercises. While on location in Florida, for instance, she was doing her usual pre-dawn running along the beach, even on the days when she faced three gruelling hours of dance rehearsals or a session with her personal trainer in the special trailer fitted out with $15,000 worth of gym equipment.

On other occasions, she would spend two hours meditating in yoga positions, achieving a deep calmness. As far as she was concerned, it was worth it. She could show anyone how to ride out life's stormiest moments, and did quite literally. One night, a loud and terrifying thunderstorm with zig-zagging lightning struck the Florida coast. While other members of the cast lay fretting in their beds, drenched in sweat, their hearts pounding, Demi went running in the rain and then took a swim in the ocean. 'She was amazing. It was almost shocking the way she handled everything,' said one of her supporting colleagues,

Siobhan Falon. Andrew Bergman agreed: 'Everything is a matter of Demi trying to have a sense of empowerment. Given her early life, you can understand it.'

The actress set up temporary home in her trailer, surrounding herself with her children. The eldest, Rumer, now seven, was also involved with the movie. She was appearing as the daughter of Demi's character. 'I thought she would give their on-screen relationship a level of reality,' Bergman told journalists. 'It's something that hasn't been seen since *Paper Moon* with Ryan and Tatum O'Neal. There was something about [Rumer's] face that reminds me of a silent movie-star; so much emotion, so much vulnerability.'

Demi agreed. She was thrilled to be working with her daughter. 'It's been a fun experience for both of us. It's also been very educational for Rumer to see what my world is really about; that it's not just dressing up, sitting in a make-up chair and getting your hair done or lipstick applied. It's something much bigger than that.' She went on: 'She's really touched me with how sweet and openly giving she is with her emotions, and how quick she gets it. How could I not have a tremendous sense of pride?'

Although she would watch some of the dance and strip routines her mother performed for the cameras, Rumer wasn't permitted to sit through all of them. One of the times she was excluded from the set was during the shooting of Demi's more provocative sequences on the stage of the film's Eager Beaver club, filmed on an interior sound stage at Miami's Greenwich Studios. One scene called for Demi, to the music of Annie Lennox's 'Money Can't Buy It', to strip down to her knickers out of the man's suit she was wearing at the start of her routine. Two hundred male extras were recruited to play the audience.

Although the fee was minimal, said one of those called up, 'There wasn't a man among us who wouldn't have done it for nothing. She was terrific.'

The decision to cast Burt Reynolds in one of the major roles was instinctive – as was his acceptance. The word around Hollywood at the time was that Reynolds was all but washed up. He was still recuperating from a bout of bad health which had had him out of action for a considerable period, and he was trying to re-establish himself.

'Burt called us up and asked to come in for an audition, which was a very brave thing for him to do,' Mike Lobell remembers, 'and when he auditioned, he had us in tears we were were laughing so much. Burt knows his character David Dilbeck because he grew up in Florida and has been around a lot of corrupt politicians.'

Reynolds couldn't agree more. 'Dilbeck is a degenerate politician who has a fixation for naked women. I know this man well for several reasons. First, my father was a chief of police in Florida for twenty years, so I was always around local politicians. Also, I've been to the White House for dinner with three different presidents. There's a lot that goes on in a politician's private life that's absolutely frightening. But that doesn't mean he's not good at his job, trying to make this country better than it is. Secondly, years ago I dated one of the premier striptease artists of her day, Lilly St Cyr.'

Although the filming of *Striptease* naturally attracted a good deal of media attention because of its subject-matter, prompted mainly by the studio publicists and the simmering anger of the Hollywood backbiters who were still smarting over Demi's $12.5 million pay day, it soon became apparent that the actress was in for a rough ride. The tabloids' treatment of her became almost as hostile as the pre-press criticism dished out on her husband's movie *Hudson Hawk*. Apart from snide speculation that if she flopped on this one she would be in trouble, the critics took the opportunity of examining her standing with the movie-going public. Several commentators remarked that a picture like *Striptease* would do nothing for her low-popularity rating among women. She lacked the qualities of warmth and vulnerability of Julia Roberts, they said, or the respect attached to the likes of Jodie Foster and Winona Ryder. Overall, she was cast as a real-life hard-faced, self-seeking bitch. *Allure* magazine, for instance, took her to task with a venomous review of her style and her tough demeanour. In a lengthy article, she was chided over her 'preternaturally perky breasts'. The writer went on to describe her as a 'famously buff mother-of-three despised by unbuff mothers-of-three everywhere'.

Speculation was heightened by leaks from the studio as the movie neared its release date. Reaction from test audiences was said to be far from encouraging. The critics hated the film. So did the studio, even though some scenes were reshot (including one, cut from the final movie, where the script called for an angry Burt Reynolds to turn violent). When it was finally released, a fairly mixed bag of reviews didn't help the unimpressive box-office figures, and only added to the confusion.

The original novel, in which the characters were funny and witty, was pretty much adhered to in the script, with the exception of Demi's character. There had been a certain amount of tampering with the role of Erin Grant, to give her a seriousness and to explain the need for her to become a striptease artist. She loses her daughter in a custody battle to her worthless husband

(Robert Patrick) and only resorts to stripping at the Eager Beaver topless bar to earn enough money to fight the case. It's where she meets her fellow strippers and bouncer Shad, played by Ving Rhames, best known at that time for his role as Marcellus Wallace in Quentin Tarantino's 1994 *Pulp Fiction* (coincidentally, with Bruce Willis in one of his greatest roles). It is also where she meets the club customers. These include Jerry Killian (William Hill) who worships Erin and who thinks he may know how to help her win her child back, and the perpetually drunk and randy Congressman, David Dilbeck (Burt Reynolds), who, although the worse for wear from the dizzy oblivion of alcohol, is still capable of leaping on stage to protect one of the dancers in mid-grind from an irritating customer. That's when the sharp-eyed Killian recognises him and initiates a blackmail plot to help Erin fund her court case. Killian, however, is discovered dead in a swamp near the outback hideaway of Detective Al Garcia (Armand Assante). The rest of the movie centres around Garcia's and Erin's attempts to track down Killian's murderers, in the course of which the detective pulls some strings in Erin's custody battle.

Although Demi's character is 'brave, heroic and stacked', she wasn't, like the other characters of Hiaasen's novel, funny. As Roger Ebert conceded, she might have been the movie's biggest downfall. 'To treat her like a plucky Sally Field heroine throws a wet blanket over the rest of the party. My guess is that when Demi Moore and the writers started musing about how Erin Grant would "really feel" in a situation, or how the audience would be able to "identify" with a mother's urge to win her child back, someone should have stepped in gently to say: "It's a comedy, honey, and when it's not a comedy, it's a satire." Everything in this movie should be for laughs, including the ex-husband, the kids and the brave Erin Grant.'

There were some undeniably excellent performances else-where, especially from Burt Reynolds, who all but single-handedly rescued the film from disaster. But, for all the hype, the miles of newsprint and Demi's own pontificating in interviews, *Striptease* was still a major let-down.

Equally disappointing was Demi's next film, Woody Allen's *Deconstructing Harry*. There were an incredible 85 speaking parts up for grabs. One of the hallmarks of Allen's movies was his recruiting the right actor for each role. Working alongside casting director Juliet Taylor, Allen admitted: 'I was very lucky to get everyone I wanted. Everyone in the film is my first choice.' At their first meeting, he handed Demi the pages of the script that pertained to her character, Helen, and told her there would be no rehearsals before principal photography began in New York on 16 September 1996, almost three months after *Striptease* had hit the screens.

She would be appearing alongside a superb and versatile ensemble of talented actors that included Kirstie Alley, Richard Benjamin, Billy Crystal, Judy Davis, Julia Louis-Dreyfus, Elisabeth Shue, Robin Williams, and of course, Allen himself. The production took just 58 days from beginning to end, and Demi's segments were shot quickly, probably in two weeks or less, with nothing more than the director's regular crew. As with every other cast member, Allen rarely offered Demi any specific directions. Instead, he would simply encourage her to explore fully the range of her own character's emotions, and it is a testament to the cast's belief in his ability that some of them didn't simply drop out of the movie there and then.

Even after Demi went home, Allen continued to work, filming sequences to be reassembled later on the cutting-room table, and at one point, the following February, he spent another six days reshooting several scenes that hadn't quite turned out the way he'd hoped they would. Almost ten months later, in December 1997, the film was scheduled for a Christmas release following its summer première and international début at the Venice Film Festival.

'Once a year, like clockwork, Woody Allen writes, directs and usually stars in exactly the film he feels like making,' began Roger Ebert's review in the *Chicago Sun-Times*. 'He works on budgets that make this possible – and just as well, given the mugging he has received from critics who think he shouldn't have made *Deconstructing Harry*.'

Although most critics praised Demi's performance, they did not much care for the movie itself. From the ones Ebert had read so far, most called it 'vulgar, smutty, profane, self-hating, self-justifying, self-involved, tasteless, bankrupt and desperate'. But in many ways, he continued, 'it is his most revealing film, his most painful, and if it also contains more than his usual quotient of big laughs, what was it the man said? "We laugh, that we may not cry." Besides, there is hardly a criticism that can be thrown at Allen that he hasn't already thrown at himself, or his alter-ego, in the film.'

As bitterly self-analytical as any of Allen's previous films, *Deconstructing Harry* was exactly as Ebert described. The story of Harry Block (Allen), a novelist whose tendency to thinly veil his own experiences in his work, as well as his unapologetic attitude and his proclivity for pills and prostitutes, has left him with three ex-wives and six former therapists. As he is about to be honoured for his writing by the college that expelled him, he faces writer's block and the impending marriage of his latest flame to a writer friend. As scenes from his stories and novels pass before his eyes and interact with him, Harry faces the people whose lives he has affected – wives, lovers, his son and his sister to name but a few.

'No single Woody Allen film ever sums up everything, or could, and what is fascinating is to watch him year after year making the most personal of films and hiding himself in plain view,' concluded Ebert.

Once again leaving herself without any time off, and as she awaited the release of *Destination Anywhere*, a short contemporary *film noir* in which she starred as Jon Bon Jovi's emotionally estranged wife, Demi's next role came knocking just as she was wrapping up her work on *Deconstructing Harry*. Screenwriter and producer Danielle Alexandra thought it was perfect for her, and that's what she told Demi when she handed over her script of *GI Jane*, inspired by the current political issues and headlines about women soldiers serving in combat.

Demi would be playing Lieutenant Jordan O'Neil, a Naval Intelligence officer adrift in her career and about to set a historic precedent when she is recruited as a test case to be the first woman allowed to train for the highly covert operations unit known as the Navy SEALs. Selected for her courage, skill and level-headedness, O'Neil is determined to succeed in the most demanding, most merciless and most honoured fighting force in the world, and survive the gruelling induction that 60 per cent of her male counterparts would fail.

Under the relentless command of Master Chief John Urgayle (Sylvester Stallone's *Daylight* co-star Viggo Mortensen), O'Neil, not expected to succeed, is put through weeks of physical and emotional hell. Certain high-ranking government and military officials, including her sponsor, Senator Lillian DeHaven (Anne Bancroft), are counting on her failing. But, much to their dismay and perplexity, she perseveres.

It's only when the recruits, on their final training exercise, are diverted to aid the evacuation of American troops from the Middle East, that O'Neil has the opportunity to prove herself, to gather all her leadership experience and courage to save the gravely wounded Master Chief and the mission – even at the risk of her own life.

Danielle Alexandra had heard through the grapevine that Demi was looking for a physically formidable role that she could get her teeth into, which was exactly what the screenwriter had in mind for the part of Lieutenant Jordan O'Neil. From day one, Alexandra explained, 'Even before I sold the project and wrote the screenplay, there was never any question that anyone other than Demi would play the role of O'Neil. I believe she was the only actress credible enough and capable of handling the physical and emotional ride. I thought of the personal and physical strength that she has as an individual, a survivor, a woman, an achiever, an actress.'

Demi was thrilled. 'I wasn't interested in just stepping into a man's character in an action movie. What *GI Jane* afforded me was the opportunity to deal not only with the enormous physical demands of the action genre, but also to be involved with something that had real substance. The story deals with subject-matter that is not only topical, but also very important, because of the bigger issue of women having more choices available to them.'

Without specifying which offers she turned down, Alexandra made it plain that Caravan Pictures' (an independent motion picture company based at the Walt Disney Studios and founded by producer Joe Roth in January 1993) was the one she simply couldn't resist, mainly because of her personal desire to work alongside Roger Birnbaum and Roth. 'When I first heard the story for this film,' Birnbaum recalled, 'it was in a pitch from Danielle. She came into our offices and I just found it all very, very exciting. It was a personal story with drama and action, and had a lot of characteristics that could attract a large audience. There's so much that goes on in this film, in terms of under-standing what the Navy SEALs are about and what they do, and the training they have to go through. It also had a lot of political intrigue as well. And Demi, quite simply, was the perfect actress for the role, because she is physically very strong and also extremely bright. Any person, whether a man or woman, who's selected to go through the Navy SEALs programme, needs to start off being a real tiger, and I think Demi is just that.'

Certainly that was the opinion of Ridley Scott of *Alien* and *Blade Runner* fame who was chosen as the director. It wasn't just the chance to work with Demi – an actress he considered to have enormous talent – that attracted him to the project, but also the film's provocative subject-matter. That, he confessed, 'would be interesting to any director'.

Casting and training the actors recruited to play the troops involved a selection procedure unlike that of most films. For instance, the so-called 'Top Forty' chosen in addition to the featured roles of the 'Great Eight' as they later came to be known, would have to face a gruelling two-week stay at a military boot camp very similar to the real thing. And, like the real thing, the aim of each actor was to shape up into perfect physical condition with the ability to speed-run over several miles, run long distances, swim at least four hundred yards (including thirty underwater) and do hundreds of sit-ups, press-ups and squat jumps.

'We took a very aggressive stance in the training programme,' recalled military technical advisor Harry Humphries. 'Stunt co-ordinator Phil Neilson and the SEAL staff were the training cadre. We tried to show the Special Forces training and the skills, including weapons-handling, that are taught in that training. We encapsulated a 17-week course into two weeks, so those actors were harassed to hell.'

Neilson agreed: 'We got them in the military frame of mind. None of these guys knew each other, and now they're buddies working together as a team and a unit.'

That team, of course, included Demi herself. 'She is a very impressive lady,' was Humphries' opinion. 'She certainly had never been put into such physical working conditions. On the first day of training, I saw this young woman out there with the rest of the troops, getting muddy doing push-ups, sit-ups and squat jumps and running around obstacles. I thought, "That's a great stunt double," so I walked up to her and said, "You've got guts." That night we were introduced, and the person I thought was the stunt double was Demi! I can't say enough about her tenacity and her will-power.'

Birnbaum agreed. 'She is one of the biggest female stars of our time, and in this movie she gets beaten up and kicked around and almost drowned. The role that Demi played was extremely demanding, one of the most challenging roles I think any actor, regardless of whether they are a man or a woman, has probably had to go through. But she is extraordinary. She put her whole heart and soul into this, and she was there every single moment for this film.'

One of those times was during the shooting of the movie's latter stages, and probably one of Demi's finest moments in the movie, when O'Neil and her group, on a training exercise, are captured and held in a simulated PoW camp, and interrogated and tortured by the Master Chief. So graphic are some of these scenes that they make for uncomfortable viewing. But Demi bristles when that scene is compared with the abuse of women. Because it's not abuse, she insists. 'In fact, I think that the Master Chief's giving O'Neil a tremendous gift putting her through her paces, and she would have been cheated if he didn't go through with it. It's not just as though he's getting back at O'Neil because he doesn't like her being there. He's doing his job. He has to deliver his men.'

She shudders at the memory of filming the subsequent scenes. Unfortunately, she laughed later, 'there was never a moment in that entire sequence where Viggo didn't get me every time! When he had me underwater, I could hear the first assistant director saying, "Let her up!" I was panicking slightly because I'd been held under for so long. And I'd said to Viggo, "Don't worry, go ahead," but I learned very quickly not to say that any more.'

The best line to deliver, she would probably agree, was when, hoisting herself up at the end of that scene, beaten to a pulp after the single-handed combat with her own commanding officer, she overwhelms her opponent and cries the words that all of us at one time or another have been tempted to scream. In the film's case, 'Suck my dick!' was enough to achieve both combat ascendancy and the respect of her fellow trainees. As *Sight and Sound* would point out, it was *GI Jane*'s answer to *Jerry Maguire*'s 'Show me the money!' All the same, it was enough to ignite America's 'Moral Majority' into a frenzy of vitriol against Walt Disney Studios, the movie's backers.

As work on the film began, the cast had to submit themselves to the brutally short Special Forces haircut. Many of them had had longish hair, and one or two even had moustaches. Only days into the initial training, Demi decided to throw a 'Shave Your Dome' party and, one after the other, the actors queued up to get cropped. 'About 10 per cent of them started just with their hair cut short,' explained Dorothy Fox, the movie's hair stylist. 'We needed to cut the rest of them right away so they could get their heads tanned, because we shot in the sun a lot and we couldn't have a bunch of red scalps.' Because the regulation cut was an eighth of an inch, Fox continued, 'we had to re-cut everyone every four days. With the Top Forty, the Great Eight, the rest of the actors, stand-ins, stunt men and the occasional extras, we did countless haircuts over those four months.'

Six weeks later, on a much-anticipated date in the shooting schedule, it was Demi's turn to shave her head to match the others. Where some actresses might consider cutting off all their hair for a film above and beyond the call of duty, Demi saw it as just another facet of the role, and was completely prepared for all that it required. As she herself explained, 'One of the big moments I thought after reading the script was the impact of the scene where O'Neil cuts her hair. It's an integral part of the story and reflects her total commitment. I had five or six months [to get used to the idea] before we reached the point of filming that scene and, when the time came, I was ready to do it in order to get on with the real down-and-dirty art of the training. I had to make it the slowest process possible because it was a one-shot deal! So I did one piece, part of the top, part of the side, and Ridley said, "Cut!" So I'm walking around now with a partially shaved head to the point where, after we'd done the second and third set-ups, I had this Hari Krishna ponytail down to my waist. It was extremely liberating.'

That was partly why she had no regrets about accepting the role, not even when she considers the pain and discomfort she experienced making the film. 'For me, it would be death to just sit where it might be safe. Either I'm a fool or have some sense of risk-taking or courage. There are too many things in life that I want to know and to taste and, as an actor, I get that kind of opportunity. If I can walk away from this film knowing just a little bit more . . . of what might be, it's mine and it has changed me for the rest of my life.'

As critic Roger Ebert correctly noted, 'Demi Moore remains one of the most adventurous of current stars, and although her films do not always succeed, she shows imagination in her choice of projects. It is also intriguing to watch her work with the image of her body. The famous pregnant photos on the cover of *Vanity Fair* can be placed beside her stripper in *Striptease*, her executive in *Disclosure* and the woman in *Indecent Proposal* who has to decide what a million dollars might purchase. All of these women, and now O'Neil, test the tension between a woman's body and a woman's ambition and will. *GI Jane* does it most obviously and effectively.'

According to the 1999 *Forbes* list of the top twenty actresses, based on three separate lists of box-office receipts, Demi was ranked eighth, just behind Drew Barrymore. The first, for total box-office gross of all her movies, was listed at just over a billion dollars, the second averaged out her top ten movies at $85 million each, and the third average, for all her movies, was around $40 million. A further survey established that four of those had grossed over $100 million. On top of that, she had retained her status as Hollywood's highest-paid actress and had ended up fifth alongside Jack Nicholson and Michael Douglas in the list of top-earning actors, just three places behind Bruce Willis, and one place, by two million, above Julia Roberts and Whoopi Goldberg – the only other female stars to figure in the same list.

As well as having been Demi's co-star in *Ghost*, and one of her Planet Hollywood allies, Goldberg was also Moore's friend and advice-giver. She, too, had a reputation for being demanding. 'There's good reason for being difficult . . . you don't get that many opportunities and when you do, you want to do it right. I've learned to say, "No, I disagree. These are the things I want." And to throw up my middle finger at those people who are wishing me ill.'

Stepping out in public, Demi would substitute for Elizabeth Taylor, who was recuperating from brain surgery and too frail to travel, at the 1997 Cannes Film Festival to chair the Cinema Against AIDS event. Demi, already in France with Willis for his *Fifth Element* international début, stood in as chairperson and host of the Miramax-sponsored event. 'I am so incredibly pleased that Demi is hosting in my place,' said Taylor from her home in Bel Air. 'She has made such important contributions towards AIDS charities and is an inspiration to all. She is a great role model and will attract much interest to this worthwhile cause.'

Ten months later, in March 1998, on the eve of the Oscars ceremony, Demi turned up alone – without Willis – at a private cocktail party in downtown Los Angeles. When the news leaked out, it was enough to send Hollywood into a frenzy of speculation. Perhaps more surprising was the fact that no one seemed to recognise her when, looking fragile and petite, she stepped out of the huge stretch limo with its darkened windows. Not even her arrival inside caused the slightest stir. While producers, writers, directors and Hollywood insiders flocked around new talents Matt Damon and Ben Affleck, and even veteran Robin Williams, to talk about their Oscar nominations for *Good Will Hunting*, Demi sat, quietly ignored and chain smoking, with a coterie of her more famous girlfriends, Madonna and bisexual Cuban nightclub owner Ingrid Casares among them, and then left again – alone. Her appearance there convinced the Hollywood gossips that what they had been suggesting for a few months was true: that she and Bruce Willis had broken up or were about to. The couple neither confirmed nor denied the rumours.

Things improved immensely for Demi as the new year got under way. Perhaps the biggest indication of her growing stature at that time was her landing a production deal with Miramax Films. Under her own Moving Pictures banner she would have a first-look deal for film and television over one year, with the option to renew for a second. 'We're not interested in developing a lot of material,' she said at the time. 'We have a few things, and what's great is that it is real group effort at Miramax.'

She found time to lend her celebrity to *Marie Claire*'s millennium issue – not as a cover girl, but as the guest editor – which was scheduled to hit the news-stands in November 1999. Previous celebrities who had sat in the editor's chair included Gwyneth Paltrow and Susan Sarandon. Asked why Demi got the job, Glenda Bailey, editor-in-chief of the American edition of the popular women's magazine, was quick to respond: because 'Demi has a great sense of style, a sense of humour and a sense of justice. She has beauty and brains.'

The actress also continued to read new scripts as they came in. The role of real-life bondage queen and 1950s pin-up beauty Bettie Page was one she was very keen on, and she was disappointed when she failed to land the part. It went instead to Willis's *Armageddon* co-star Liv Tyler. This wasn't the first time Demi had lost out on a role she wanted. 'The most "out there" I've gone to get a film was for *Sleepless in Seattle*. Someone got me a copy of the script and I loved it. Whatever part of my fucked-up psychology it has to do with, I don't like to put myself out there like this, but I called the head of Tristar and said, "I want to do this!" I don't like feeling that vulnerable. Sometimes, roles I've wanted have floated right by me, and I've thought, "Things that are meant to be are meant to be." Anyway, on *Sleepless in Seattle*, they were very nice, respectful, pleasant, but obviously, I got rejected. They wanted Meg Ryan.'

*Batman Returns* and *Basic Instinct* were a couple of other films she would like to have done, she remembers. 'I really wanted to do *Basic Instinct*, but Paul Verhoeven [the director] wouldn't even see me for the part. And I was even blonde at the time! Sharon Stone was really great in it, though. What struck me about that character was that she was a woman in control of her life, however "sick" it was. So many times in movies where's there's blatant sex, it's as if it's being *done* to the woman. The sexiest moment in *Basic Instinct*, the one that reminded me how much I had wanted that part, was the interrogation scene where Sharon Stone parted her legs. I thought, "Great!" I guess, unlike a lot of people in this country, I never question whether something's pornographic or offensive. I loved the power of that moment.'

She did not have to dwell too long on the roles she'd missed out on, however. Something awaited her just around the corner.

According to *Daily Variety* reports, she was the front runner for Alain Berliner's *Passion of Mind*. Based on a screenplay by Ron Bass (who wrote *My Best Friend's Wedding*) and originally developed for Michelle Pfeiffer, the script had been doing the Hollywood rounds for close on a decade, and in that time had been eyed by Nicole Kidman, Meg Ryan and Winona Ryder among others. In the end, Demi did indeed land the leading role – both of them.

According to a synopsis that appeared on the internet several months before filming got under way, *Passion of Mind* was a psychological romantic drama in which fantasy and reality become indistinguishable for a woman leading a double life in her dreams. One of Demi's dual characters, Marie, is a beautiful but lonely American widow living with two daughters in the South of France who creates an imaginary existence in her dreams. But is she really Marie, or is she Demi's other character, Marty, a glamorous New York career woman dreaming of a life in Provence? Reluctant to reveal their increasing confusion to the men in their lives, played by Stellan Skargaard and William Fichtner, Marie and Marty must quickly discover which life is real and which is a dream, before they both lose everything.

According to the *Globe, Star* and *National Enquirer*, Demi and Dennis Bridwell, a security guard on the set in France, were looking a lot closer than two people who happened to be working on a movie set together. At Demi's 36th birthday party in Provence that November, one of those ubiquitous 'friends' who always seem to be on hand to comment upon showbiz affairs of the heart, revealed that the restaurant staff were a-twitter at how close the two looked. They were 'holding hands when it appeared no one was looking'. But none of that was true. It was something

Demi's spokesperson, Pat Kingsley, reinforced when she talked to the *New York Daily News*. 'She doesn't have a romantic relationship with anyone. Period.' Demi just let the speculation drift over her head.

Two months earlier, Britain's *Now* magazine had reported that 'Demi Moore appears to have put the final nail in the coffin of her marriage to Bruce Willis by moving her new lover, Olivier Whitcomb, into a cottage on her estate in Idaho.' Ironically, it was Willis who introduced Demi to Whitcomb in the first place some years previously when he'd coached the actor in martial arts. Although Demi and Whitcomb would see more of each other after her marriage had ended, there was never any basis to suggestions that the couple were anything more than just friends at that time. It was only after her hopes of a reconciliation with Willis were dashed, and Bruce moved in with his new love, another Demi lookalike Maria Bravo, that Demi and Whitcomb became an item. Or at least, that's the speculation. Not that Demi had anything to say on the subject, and neither for that matter had Whitcomb. But whoever she chooses to spend her future with, and whatever she chooses to do in the career that stretches out before her, it's guaranteed that her instincts will remain sharp and her abilities will remain undiminished.

As Demi celebrates her second decade in the entertainment industry, it is clear that she has established herself among the world's top film stars. Even when her movies were bad, her abilities as an actress still shone through. Breaking with its critical observation and earlier opinions the authoritative *Sight and Sound* magazine admitted, 'She has honed an ability to appeal to men and woman in equal measure: if male viewers want to have her, female viewers want to be her – or vice versa.

Either way, both want to watch her. She is in many ways the perfect multiplex product, maximising audiences across gender lines.' On top of that, most would admit, she has traded the small, challenging and artistically risky roles for huge salaries and big blockbusters and recognises that the key to her own success is tighter control over her own destiny whether on or off the screen.

As journalist Sally Kline noted, 'Studying Demi Moore sitting next to you in Manhattan's Four Seasons Hotel, you are immediately struck by the contradictions. She's dressed in a way at once brazenly sexy and who-cares comfortable. Snug Levi's. Man-tailored black satin shirt unbuttoned down to there. She's tiny, ladylike, skinny. Yet she sits in the straight-backed chair with her legs wide apart. She owns her own space, resisting the inherently defensive posture of the interviewee. And the boots. The heels of the expensive fashion-forward leather boots say it all: toweringly high the way a man likes them, but square and thick and sturdy so that a woman can walk.'

Demi's consummate stardom is partly rooted in the way she has manipulated the boundary between her screen and private self. Her approach is reminiscent of old Hollywood exploitation in that she places her real self as a commodity adjacent to the celluloid image, the two to be modelled, marketed and advertised as one. From that point of view, Demi Moore is undoubtedly a quick-change artist whose famously naked flesh is only one of her cloaks.

It is what makes her so fascinating. It is also what makes a movie star.

# FILMOGRAPHY

*Choices* (1981)

90 minutes

Directed by Silvio Narizzano

Cast: Val Avery, Pat Buttram, Paul Carafotes, Victor French, Lelia Goldoni, Art Kimbro, Demi Moore, William R. Moses, Stephen Nichols, Dennis Patrick, Don Stark

*Young Doctors in Love* (1982)

92 minutes

Directed by Garry Marshall

Screenplay by Michael Elias and Rich Eustis

Production Company: 20th Century Fox

Cast: Sean Young (Dr Stephanie Brody), Michael McKean (Dr Simon August), Gary Friedkin (Dr Milton Chamberlain), Kyle T. Heffner (Dr Charles Litto), Rick Overton (Dr Thurman Flicker), Crystal Bernard (Julie), Ted McGinley (Dr Bucky DeVol), Saul Rubinek (Floyd Kurtzman), Harry Dean Stanton (Dr Oliver Ludwig), Pamela Reed (Nurse Norine Sprockett),

Taylor Negron (Dr Phil Burns), Patrick Collins (Dr Walter Rist), Dabney Coleman (Dr Joseph Prang), Titos Vandis (Sal Bonafetti), Michael Richards (Malamud), Demi Moore (New Intern)

*Parasite* (1982)
85 minutes
Directed by Charles Band
Screenplay by Alan J. Adler and Frank Levering
Production Company: Embassy Pictures Corporation
Cast: Robert Glaudini (Dr Paul Dean), Demi Moore (Patricia Welles), Luca Bercovici (Ricus), James Davidson (Merchant), Al Fann (Collins), Tom Villard (Zeke), Scott Thomson (Chris), Cherie Currie (Dana), Vivian Blaine (Miss Daley), James Cavan (Buddy), Joannelle Nadine Romero (Bo), Freddie Moore (Arn), Natalie May (Shell)

*No Small Affair* (1984)
102 minutes
Directed by Jerry Schatzberg
Screenplay by Charles Bolt and Terence Mulcahy
Cast: Jon Cryer (Charles Cummings), Demi Moore (Laura Victor), George Wendt (Jake), Peter Frechette (Leonard), Elizabeth Daily (Susan), Ann Wedgeworth (Joan Cummings), Jeffrey Tambor (Ken), Tim Robbins (Nelson), Hamilton Camp (Gus Sosnowski), Scott Getlin (Scott), Judith Baldwin (Stephanie), Jennifer Tilly (Mona), Kene Holliday (Walt Cronin)
US Box Office: $5,000,000

*Master Ninja 1* (1984)

Directed by Ray Austin and Robert Clouse

Production Company: Film Ventures International

Cast: Claude Akins (Mr Trumbull), Charles Collins, Clu
Culgar Collins (Mr Christiansen), Sho Kosugi (Okasa), Lori
Lethin, Bill McKinney, Demi Moore (Holly Trumbull), Lee
Van Cleef (The Master: John Peter McAlister), Timothy Van
Patten (Max Keller)

*Blame it on Rio* (1984)

100 minutes

Directed by Stanley Donen

Screenplay by Charlie Peters and Larry Gelbart

Production Company: Sherwood

Cast: Michael Caine (Matthew Hollis), Joseph Bologna (Victor
Lyons), Valerie Harper (Karen Hollis), Michelle Johnson
(Jennifer Lyons), Demi Moore (Nicole Hollis), Jose Lewgoy
(Eduardo Marques), Lupe Giglioti (Signora Botega), Michel
Manaugh (Peter), Tessy Callado (Helaine)

US Box Office: $18,600,000

*St Elmo's Fire* (1985)

110 minutes

Directed by Joel Schumacher

Screenplay by Joel Schumacher and Carl Kurlander

Production Company: Columbia Pictures

Cast: Emilio Estevez (Kirbo), Robert Lowe (Billy), Andrew
McCarthy (Kevin), Demi Moore (Jules), Judd Nelson (Alex),
Ally Sheedy (Leslie), Mare Winningham (Wendy), Martin
Balsam (Mr Beamish), Andie MacDowell (Dale Biberman),

Joyce Van Patten (Mrs Beamish), Jenny Wright (Felicia), Blake
Clark (Wally), Jon Cutler (Howard Krantz)
US Box Office: $37,800,000

*Wisdom* (1986)
109 minutes
Directed and written by Emilio Estevez
Production Company: Gladden Entertainment
Cast: Demi Moore (Karen Simmons), Emilio Estevez (John
Wisdom), Tom Skerritt (Lloyd Wisdom), Veronica Cartwright
(Samantha Wisdom), William Allen Young (Williamson),
Richard Michemberg (Cooper), Ernie Brown (Hotel Manager),
Bill Henderson (Theo), Gene Ross (Sheriff), Liam Silver (Luke
Perry), Charlie Sheen (City Burger Manager)
US Box Office: $5,715,000

*One Crazy Summer* (1986)
89 minutes
Directed and written by Savage Steve Holland
Production Company: A&M/Warner Brothers
Cast: John Cusack (Hoops McCann), Demi Moore
(Cassandra), Curtis Armstrong (Ack Ack Raymond), William
Hickey (Old Man Beckersted), Joe Flaherty (General
Raymond), Tom Villard (Clay Stork), Billie Bird (Grandma),
John Matuszak (Stan), Mark Metcalf (Aquilla Beckersted),
Kimberly Foster (Cookie Campbell), Joel Murray (George
Calamari)
US Box Office: $13,431,000

*About Last Night* (1986)

113 minutes

Directed by Edward Zwick

Screenplay by Denise DeClue and Tim Kazurinsky

Production Company: Metro-Goldwyn-Mayer

Cast: Rob Lowe (Danny), Demi Moore (Debbie), James Belushi (Bernie), Elizabeth Perkins (Joan), George DiCenzo (Mr Favio), Michael Alldredge (Mother Malone), Robin Thomas (Steve Carlson), Donna Gibbons (Alex), Megan Mullaly (Pat), Patricia Duff (Leslie), Rosanna DeSoto (Mrs Lyons), Sachi Parker (Carrie), Robert Neches (Gary), Joe Greco (Gus), Ada Maris (Carmen)

US Box Office: $38,702,000


*The Seventh Sign* (1988)

97 minutes

Directed by Carl Schultz

Screenplay by George Kaplan and W.W. Wicket

Production Company: Interscope Communications/Tristar Pictures

Cast: Demi Moore (Abby Quinn), Michael Biehn (Russell Quinn), Jurgen Prochnow (David Bannon), Peter Friedmans (Father Lucci), Manny Jacobs (Avi), Johnny Taylor (Jimmy Szaragosa), Lee Garlington (Dr Inness), Akosua Busia (Penny)

US Box Office: $18,875,000


*We're No Angels* (1989)

101 minutes

Directed by Neil Jordan

Screenplay by David Mamet

Production Company: Paramount Pictures
Cast: Robert DeNiro (Ned), Sean Penn (Jim), Demi Moore
(Molly), Hoyt Axton (Father Levesque), Bruno Kirby
(Deputy), Ray McAnally (Warden), James Russo (Bobby),
Wallace Shawn (Translator), John C. Reilly (Young Monk), Jay
Brazeau (Sherriff), Ken Buhay (Bishop Nogalich), Elizabeth
Lawrence (Mrs Blair), Bill Murdoch (deputy), Jessica Jickels
(Rosie)
US Box Office: $10,555,000

*Ghost* (1990)
128 minutes
Directed by Jerry Zucker
Screenplay by Bruce Joel Rubin
Production Company: Paramount Pictures
Cast: Patrick Swayze (Sam Wheat), Demi Moore (Molly
Jensen), Tony Goldwyn (Carl Bruner), Stanley Lawrence
(Elevator Man), Christopher J Keene (Elevator Man), Susan
Breslau (Susan), Martina Degnam (Rose), Richard Kleber
(Mover), Macka Foley (Mover), Rick Aviles (Willie Lopez),
Phil Leeds (Emergency Room Ghost), John Hugh (Surgeon),
Sam Tsoutsouvas (Minister), Sharon Beslau Cornell (Cemetery
Ghost), Vincent Schiavelli (Subway Ghost), Angelina Estrad
(Roas Santiago), Whoopi Goldberg (Oda Mae Brown), Armelia
McQueen (Oda Mae's Sister), Gail Boggs (Oda Mae's Sister)
US Box Office: $217,631,000

*Nothing But Trouble* (1991)
94 minutes
Directed and written by Dan Aykroyd

Production Company: Warner Brothers

Cast: Chevy Chase (Chris Throne), Dan Aykroyd (J.P./Bobo), John Candy (Denis/Eldona), Demi Moore (Diane Lightson), Valri Bromfield (Miss Purdah), Taylor Negron (Fausto), Bertila Damas (Renalda), Raymond J. Barry (Mark), Brian Doyle-Murray (Brian), John Wesley (Sam)

US Box Office: $8,479,000

*The Butcher's Wife* (1991)

107 minutes

Directed by Terry Hughes

Screenplay by Ezra Litwak and Marjorie Schwartz

Production Company: Paramount Pictures

Cast: Demi Moore (Marina), Jeff Daniels (Alex), George Dzundza (Leo), Mary Steenburgen (Stella), Frances McDormand (Grace), Margaret Colin (Robyn), Max Perlich (Eugene), Miriam Margolyes (Gina), Helen Hanft (Molly), Christopher Durang (Mr Liddle), Luis Avalos (Luis)

US Box Office: $9,689,000

*Mortal Thoughts* (1991)

103 minutes

Directed by Alan Rudolph

Screenplay by Claude Kerven and William Reilly

Production Company: Columbia Pictures

Cast: Demi Moore (Cynthia Kellogg), Glenne Headly (Joyce Urbanski), Bruce Willis (James Urbanski), John Pankow (Arthur Kellogg), Harvey Keitel (Det. John Woods), Billie Neal (Linda Nealon), Frank Vincent (Dominic Marino), Karen Shallo (Gloria Urbanski), Crystal Field (Jeanette Marino),

Marianne Leone (Aunt Rita)
US Box Office: $19,018,000

*A Few Good Men* (1992)
138 minutes
Directed by Rob Reiner
Screenplay by Aaron Sorkin
Production Company: Castle Rock Entertainment/Columbia
Pictures
Cast: Tom Cruise (Lt Daniel Kaffee), Jack Nicholson (Col
Nathan R. Jessep), Demi Moore (Lt Cmdr JoAnne Galloway),
Kevin Bacon (Capt Jack Ross), Kiefer Sutherland (Lt Jonathan
Kendrick), Kevin Pollack (Lt Sam Weinberg), James Marshall
(Pfc Louden Downey), J.T. Walsh (Lt Col. Matthew Markin-
son), Christopher Guest (Doctor Stones), J.A. Preston (Judge
Randolph), Matt Craven (Lt Dave Spradling), Wolfgang
Bodison (Lance Cprl Harold W. Dawson), Xander Berkeley
(Capt Whitaker), John M. Jackson (Capt West), Noah Wyle
(Cpl Jeffrey Barnes)
Fee: $3,000,000
US Box Office: $141,340,000

*Indecent Proposal* (1993)
117 minutes
Directed by Adrian Lyne
Screenplay by Jack Engelhard and Amy Holden Jones
Production Company: Paramount Pictures
Cast: Robert Redford (John Cage), Demi Moore (Diana
Murphy), Woody Harrelson (David Murphy), Seymour Cassel
(Mr Shackleford), Oliver Platt (Jeremy), Rip Taylor (Mr Lang-

ford), Billy Connolly (Auction Emcee), Joel Brooks (Realtor),
Pierre Epstein (Van Buren), Danny Zorn (Screenwriter), Kevin
West (Screenwriter), Pamela Holt (David's Girlfriend), Tommy
Bash (David's Father), Mariclare Costello (David's Mother)
US Box Office: $106,614,000

*A Century of Cinema* (1994)
72 minutes
Directed by Caroline Thomas
Written by Bob Thomas
Cast: Richard Attenborough, Dan Aykroyd, Kim Basinger,
Milton Berle, George Burns, Tim Burton, Nicholas Cage,
Kevin Costner, Billy Crystal, Tony Curtis, Joe Dante, Kirk
Douglas, Robert Downey Jr, Clint Eastwood, Sally Field, Jane
Fonda, Harrison Ford, Morgan Freeman, Charlton Heston,
Bob Hope, Anthony Hopkins, Bob Hoskins, Demi Moore,
Maureen O'Hara, Vincent Price, Dennis Quaid, Burt Reynolds,
Julia Roberts, Mickey Rooney, Meg Ryan, Steven Spielberg,
Sylvester Stallone, James Stewart, Meryl Streep, Donald
Sutherland (all as themselves)

*Disclosure* (1994)
128 minutes
Directed by Barry Levinson
Screenplay by Michael Crichton and Paul Attanasio
Production Company: Warner Brothers
Cast: Michael Douglas (Tom Sanders), Demi Moore (Meredith
Johnson), Donald Sutherland (Bob Garvin), Caroline Goodall
(Susan Hendler), Roma Maffia (Catherine Alvarez), Dylan
Baker (Philip Blackburn), Rosemary Forsyth (Stephanie

Kaplan), Dennis Miller (Mark Lewyn), Suzie Plakson (Mary Anne Hunter), Nicholas Sadler (Don Cherry), Jacqui Kim (Cindy Chang), Joe Urla (John Conley Jr), Michael Chieffo (Stephen Chase)
Fee: $5,000,000
US Box Office: $83,000,000

*The Scarlet Letter* (1995)
135 minutes
Directed by Roland Joffe
Screenplay by Douglas Day Stewart based on the novel by Nathaniel Hawthorne
Production Company: Moving Pictures/Cinergi
Cast: Demi Moore (Hester Prynne), Gary Oldman (Reverend Arthur Dimmesdale), Robert Duvall (Dr Roger Prynne), Lisa Jolliff-Andoh (Mituba), Edward Hardwicke (John Bellingham), Robert Prosky (Horace Stonehall), Roy Dotrice (Thomas Cheever), Joan Plowright (Harriet Hibbons), Malcolm Storry (Major Dusmuir), James Beardon (Goodman Mortimer), Larissa Lapchinksi (Goody Mortimer), Amy Wright (Goody Gotwick), George Aguilar (Johnny Sassamon), Tim Woodward (Brewster Stonehall), Joan Gregson (Elizabeth Cheever)
US Box Office: $10,400,000

*Now and Then* (1995)
96 minutes
Directed by Lesli Linka Glatter
Screenplay by I. Marlene King
Production Company: New Line Cinema
Cast: Christina Ricci (Young Roberta), Thora Birch (Young

Teeny), Gaby Hoffmann (Young Samantha), Ashleigh Aston
Moore (Young Chrissy), Demi Moore (Samantha), Rosie
O'Donnell (Roberta), Rita Wilson (Chrissy), Melanie Griffith
(Teeny), Rumer Willis (Angela Albertson), Bonnie Hunt (Mrs
Dewitt), Devon Sawa (Scott Wormer), Travis Robertson
(Wormer brother), Justin Humphrey (Wormer brother),
Bradley Coyyell (Wormer brother), Janeane Garofalo
(Wiladene)
US Box Office: $27,400,000

*The Juror* (1996)
118 minutes
Directed by Brian Gibson
Screenplay by George Dawes Green and Ted Tally
Production Company: Columbia Pictures
Cast: Demi Moore (Annie Laird), Alec Baldwin (Teacher),
Joseph Gordon-Levitt (Oliver), Anne Heche (Juliet), James
Gandolfini (Eddie), Lindsay Crouse (Tallow), Tony Lo Bianco
(Louie Boffano), Michael Constantine (Judge Weitzel), Matt
Craven (Boone), Todd Susman (Bozeman), Michael Rispoli
(Joseph Boffano), Julie Halston (Inez), Frank Adonis
(DeCicco), Matthew Cowles (Rodney)
Fee: $7,000,000
US Box Office: $44,834,000

*The Hunchback of Notre Dame* (1996)
90 minutes
Directed by Gary Trousdale and Kirk Wise
Screenplay by Irene Mecchi based on the novel by Victor Hugo
Production Company: Walt Disney/Buena Vista

Voice-over cast: Tom Hulce (Quasimodo), Demi Moore
(Esmeralda), Tony Jay (Frollo), Kevin Kline (Phoebus), Paul
Kandel (Clopin), Jason Alexander (Hugo), Charles Kimbrough
(Victor), Mary Wickes (Laverne), David Ogden Stiers (The
Archdeacon), Heidi Mollenhauer (Esmeralda [singing]), Mary
Kay Bergman (Quasimodo's Mother), Corey Burton (Brutish
Guard)
US Box Office: $100,117,000


*Beavis and Butthead Do America* (1996)
80 minutes
Directed by Mike Judge and Yvette Kaplan
Screenplay by Mike Judge
Production Company: Paramount Pictures
Voice-over cast: Mike Judge (Beavis/Butt-head/Tom Anderson/
Mr Van Driessen/Principal McVicker), Robert Stack (FBI
Agent Flemming), Cloris Leachman (Martha), Jacqueline
Barba (Agent Hurly), Pamela Blair (Flight Attendant/White
House Tour Guide), Eric Bogosian (Ranger), Kristofor Brown
(Man on Plane/Second Man in Confession Booth/Old Guy/
Jim), Tony Darling (Motley Crue Roadie #2/Tourist Man),
John Donman (Airplane Captain/White House Representative),
Francis Dumaurier (French Dignitary), Jim Flaherty (Petrified
Forest Recording), Tim Guinee (Hoover Guide/ATF Agent),
David Letterman (Motley Crue Roadie #1), Toby Huss (TV
Chief #2/Concierge/Bellboy/Male TV Reporter), Sam Johnson
(Limo Driver/TV Chief #1/Man in Confession Booth #1/
Petrified Forest Ranger), Demi Moore (Dallas Grimes)

*Striptease* (1996)

115 minutes

Directed by Andrew Bergman

Screenplay by Carl Hiaasen and Andrew Bergman

Production Company: Castle Rock Entertainment

Cast: Demi Moore (Erin Grant), Burt Reynolds (Congressman
David Dilbeck), Armand Assante (Lieutenant Al Garcia), Ving
Rhames (Shad), Robert Patrick (Darrell Grant), Paul Guilfoyle
(Malcolm Moldovsky), Jerry Grayson (Orly), Rumer Willis
(Angela Grant), Robert Stanton (Erb Crandal), William Hill
(Jerry Killian), Stuart Pamkin (Alan Mordecai), Dina Spybey
(Monique Jr), PaSean Wilspon (Sabrina Hepburn), Pandora
Preaks (Urbanna Sprawl), Barbara Alyn Woods (Lorelei)

Fee: $12,500,000

US Box Office: $32,758,000

*Deconstructing Harry* (1997)

95 minutes

Directed and written by Woody Allen

Production Company: Fine Line Features

Cast: Woody Allen (Harry Block), Caroline Aaron (Doris),
Kirstie Alley (Joan), Bob Balaban (Richard), Richard Benjamin
(Ken), Eric Bogosian (Burt), Billy Crystal (Larry), Judy Davis
(Lucy), Hazelle Goodman (Cookie), Mariel Hemingway (Beth
Kramer), Amy Irving (Jane), Eric Lloyd (Hilly Block), Julia
Louis-Dreyfus (Leslie), Tobey Maguire (Harvey Stern), Demi
Moore (Helen), Julie Kavner (Grace), Elisabeth Shue (Fay),
Stanley Tucci (Paul Epstein), Robin Williams (Mel).

Fee: $450,000

US Box Office: $10,569,000

*Destination Anywhere* (1997)

45 minutes

Directed by Marl Pellington

Screenplay by Stuart Cohin and Tom Gorai

Production Company: Blue Goose

Cast: Jon Bon Jovi (Jon), Demi Moore (Janie), Annabella Sciorra (Dorothy), Kevin Bacon (Mike), Whoopi Goldberg (Cabbie), Leah Rubino (Ghost Girl), Nicky 'Pop' Anest (Leo's Lips), Olga Barbato (Bella), Vinny Bella (Angry Window Man), Sidney Annis (Domino Man #1), Erinie Fierron (Domino Man #2), Denise Faye (Main Stripper), Paul D'Amato (Preacher), William Preston (Homeless Man), Harry Bugin (Bartender)

*GI Jane* (1997)

124 minutes

Directed by Ridley Scott

Screenplay by Danielle Alexandra and David N. Twohy

Production Company: First Independent/Moving Pictures

Cast: Demi Moore (Lt Jordan O'Neil), Viggo Mortensen (Master Chief John Urgayle), Anne Bancroft (Senator Lillian Dehaven), Jason Beghe (Royce), Daniel Von Bargen (Theodore Hayes), John Michael Higgins (Chief of Staff), Kevin Gage (Instructor Pyro), David Warshofsky (Instructor Johns), David Vadim (Cortez), Morris Chestnut (McCool), Josh Hopkins (Flea), James Cavielzel (Slovnik), Boyd Kestner (Wickwire), Angel David (Newburry), Stephen Ramsey (Stamm)

Fee: $11,000,000

US Box Office: $48,154,000

*Passion of Mind* (1999)

Directed by Alain Berliner

Screenplay by Ronald Bass and David Field

Production Company: Paramount Classics

Cast: Demi Moore (Marty/Marie), Matthew Beisner, Sinead Cusack, William Fichtner, Peter Riegert, Stellan Skarsgaard

## TELEVISION

*General Hospital* (1982–83)

*The Master* (1984) – episode: 'Max'

*Bedrooms* (1984) – TV movie

*Moonlighting* (1985) – episode: 'When Girls Collide'

*The New Homeowner's Guide to Happiness* (1988) – TV Special

*Tales from the Crypt* (1990) – episode: 'Dead Right'

*If These Walls Could Talk* (1996) – TV movie

*Ellen* (1997) – episode: 'The Puppy Episode'

*City Kids Speak: Celebration!* – host for TV Special

## THEATRE

*The Early Girl* (1987) – New York stage performance

## PRODUCER

*City Kids Speak: Celebration!* – TV Special (co-producer)

*Mortal Thoughts* (1991) (co-producer)

*The Scarlet Letter* (1995)

*Now and Then* (1995)

*If These Walls Could Talk* (1996) (executive producer)

*GI Jane* (1997)

*Austin Powers: International Man of Mystery* (1997) (co-producer)

*Austin Powers: The Spy Who Shagged Me* (1999) (co-producer)

## NOMINATIONS AND AWARDS

### Golden Globe

*Ghost* (1991)

Nominated for Best Actress

*If These Walls Could Talk* (1997)

Nominated for Best Performance by an actress in a mini-series or motion picture made for TV

### MTV Movie Awards

*A Few Good Men* (1993)

Nominated for Best Female Performance

*Indecent Proposal* (1994)

Winner of Best Kiss

Nominated for Best Female Performance

*Disclosure* (1995)

Nominated for Best Villain and Most Desirable Female

*The Scarlet Letter* (1996)

Nominated for Most Desirable Female

*GI Jane* (1998)

Nominated for Best Fight

### Miscellaneous

*The Early Girl* (1987)

Winner of Theatre World Award

People's Choice Awards (1993)

Winner of Favourite Dramatic Motion Picture Actress

ShoWest Awards (1994)

Winner of Female Star of the Year